THE
COMSTOCK
PAPERS

THE
COMSTOCK
PAPERS

By Henry DeGroot

Introduction by David Thompson

A Publication of
THE GRACE DANGBERG FOUNDATION

DANGBERG HISTORICAL SERIES

Donald Dickerson, Editor

Copyright 1985 by The Grace Dangberg Foundation, Inc.,
P.O. Box 9621 University Station, Reno, Nevada 89507.

Library of Congress Catalog No. 85-80913

ISBN 0-913205-08-7

Cover by Bill Barker

CONTENTS

XX

INTRODUCTION

By David Thompson

The Comstock Papers, written by Henry DeGroot and published in the *Mining & Scientific Press* during the latter half of 1876, is an important primary source of early Nevada history. DeGroot was a jack-of-all-trades who witnessed at first hand the "Rush to Washoe" and the beginning of mining on the Comstock Lode in 1859.

The Comstock Lode was a mass of silver and gold ore which produced hundreds of millions of dollars in profits for its owners. Its wealth built much of nineteenth century San Francisco and created some of the great fortunes of the age. The Comstock dominated the rest of Nevada's politics, economics and society from the time of its discovery until the turn of the century. The Lode was internationally famous for its richness, and for the hotels, foundries, banks, and railroads which it built.

Virginia City and Gold Hill, the twin cities of the Comstock, attracted tens of thousands of people to live there. During the nineteenth century, Virginia City was by far the largest town in the state of Nevada. The place was internationally famous for its huge stamp mills and its mazelike caverns, chambers, passageways, and shafts.

In *The Comstock Papers,* DeGroot describes the original discoveries of the fantastically rich Comstock Lode, and how it got its name. He traces the strange fates of the pioneer locators on the Lode and regales the reader with tales of the unusual characters who exploited its riches. Written during the heyday of Virginia City and Gold Hill, *The Comstock Papers* fills a unique position in the annals of Nevada.

The author of *The Comstock Papers* is almost as interesting as the saga of the mighty Lode. Henry DeGroot was born in 1815, on a farm in eastern New

York. DeGroot's father died when Henry was still a boy, leaving little in the way of an estate except debts. The family had enough money for DeGroot to go to school, however, and he earned a degree from Union College in Schenectady, New York. He graduated in May, 1841, when he was about sixteen years old.

DeGroot then took up the study of law and was admitted to practice in his native state. According to his friend Frederick E. Birge, who wrote an appreciation of DeGroot in the *Overland Monthly* in 1893, "Later he studied medicine, but finding the practice of this profession only experimenting with the lives of men, he wholly abandoned it, though the title of Doctor clung to him."

He married seventeen-year old Eliza Mead of Saratoga County, New York, an educated and accomplished young lady, and together the two of them took charge of a seminary for young ladies in Ossining, Westchester County, New York, along the scenic Hudson River.

DeGroot loved to write articles for newspapers and was a personal friend of Horace Greeley, the controversial editor of the New York *Tribune* and later candidate for the Presidency of the United States. When gold was discovered in California at the beginning of 1848, Greeley asked DeGroot to go to California and furnish the readers of the *Tribune* with the latest and most reliable information on the ore strike. DeGroot, leaving his wife and child in New York, traveled to California by sailing ship and landed at Yerba Buena before the year ended.

DeGroot immediately went to Sutter's Mill, now the town of Coloma on the American River, where the first nuggets were found. After talking to the discoverers, he went on a prospecting expedition into the mountains, described by Frederick Birge: "Of course, only a prophetic vision could at that time foresee the extent and importance of the discovery of gold. Those who were there when the first discovery was made had no idea as to whether it was a local discovery or not; and if local, whether it was extensive enough to be of any great value. It appears, however, that the Doctor got about that portion of the country with pick, pan, and shovel, and by actual demonstration satisfied himself that the greatest gold field ever known had been found. The labor of this demonstration was handsomely rewarded by the product in dust and nuggets.

On this excursion his companion was John F. Pinkham, now a resident of San Francisco. They traveled on foot into wholly unknown country and among troublesome savages. They got back to Sutter's Mill on the Fourth of July, 1849. At this time a considerable number of men had congregated about Sutter's Mill, and it was the common sentiment that the day must be properly celebrated. This, however, involved an oration. Upon a canvass no one was found who could or would supply this, until Mr. Pinkham declared that his partner was emminently qualified, and lacked only a disposition to put himself forward. This brought out the first Fourth of July oration delivered in the State, and it is said to have been enthusiastically appreciated.''

Not long afterwards DeGroot returned to New York and brought his wife Eliza and their baby to California. He became an authority on hydraulic mining and kept up a stream of correspondence to the New York *Tribune*. Later, he went to work for the San Francisco *Alta California* and wrote stories and articles for them for years.

In 1859, DeGroot was one of the first newspapermen on the scene to cover the story of the discovery of the Comstock Lode in what was then western Utah Territory. He lived in Gold Canyon, where he met most of the early discoverers of the Lode and became acquainted with the principal characters in the area. He later wrote *The Comstock Papers,* reprinted in this volume, as a recollection and history of the first years of mining in the Lode for the *Mining and Scientific Press* in 1876. Grant H. Smith, the author of the 1943 work *The History of the Comstock Lode 1850-1920,* said of *The Comstock Papers,* "We are indebted to Henry DeGroot for the names of the locators of the principal Comstock mines, most of whom were Gold

Canyon placer miners."

In the spring of 1860, DeGroot collaborated with the well-known western writer and humorist J. Ross Browne in writing letters to the New York *Times* and San Francisco *Bulletin* about conditions on the Comstock. According to Charles Howard Shinn, who penned *The Story of the Mine, As Illustrated by the Great Comstock Lode of Nevada,* DeGroot and Browne lived "in a hole in the hillside." That year DeGroot wrote "Sketches of the Washoe Silver Mines," a pamphlet published in San Francisco. It was the first published work on a subject later treated by hundreds of books, essays, articles, and stories. DeGroot also made the pioneer map of the region in 1860, a chart entitled "Map of the Washoe Silver Mines." Both these works were later included in J. Wells Kelly's *First Directory of Nevada Territory,* published in 1862. According to Shinn, the "versatile" Doctor DeGroot wrote the text of the *First Directory* for Kelly.

DeGroot was doing more than just writing. The *Index to the Records of Carson County* shows that he was a partner in the purchase and sale of lots in Carson City during 1860. That same year he surveyed a wagon road between Double Springs and "Esmeralda" (later the town of Aurora) on the Walker River and was employed to lay out a railroad route between Carson City and the Comstock. DeGroot also owned property in and near Dayton. By 1861 he was the proprietor of a toll road and a partner with H. M. Yerington and others in a big wood ranch eight miles south of Genoa.

DeGroot was appointed by proclamation on July 24, 1861, to take the first census of Nevada Territory—a job which he successfully completed. Unfortunately for DeGroot, he seems to have run afoul of William Morris Stewart, the territorial legislator from Carson City and later Nevada's first U.S. Senator. As a result, DeGroot wasn't paid for his services as census marshal in a parliamentary maneuver which Territorial Councilman Tom Hannah suggested should have been titled "An Act to prevent Henry DeGroot from receiving his pay."

The Territorial Legislature also employed Henry

DeGroot by joint resolution to prepare a map of Nevada Territory on the scale of ten miles to the inch. It was to be completed within ten days and paid for by an unspecified sum of money. The "very neat little map" was later referred to by the Legislature as having been given to them gratuitously, indicating DeGroot wasn't paid for that either.

Perhaps it was in the cards. DeGroot's friend Birge noted that the Doctor was an indefatigable worker but not a money-maker. As Birge remarked: "The detail of business cares was very distasteful to him. He could and did furnish the information, and to a large extent the brains, on which others built fame and financial success — services that were seldom appreciated substantially."

As a result, DeGroot returned to writing for newspapers and publishers. Although there are stock certificates extant for a mining company named after him and dated 1863, he moved to Nye County, Nevada. There he and publisher Joseph E. Eckley began printing the county's first newspaper, the *Nye County News,* at Ione. It had a brief life; the Republican journal began its press run in late June of 1864 and suspended publication that autumn.

He apparently did a lot of "ghostwriting," according to Birge: "Much of Doctor DeGroot's work will live as long as a history of the Pacific States is preserved. He did much to make history and more to record it. He did much the larger part of the work of producing several volumes that are very widely known but published under other names. His work of this character was for the most part done under the pressure of poverty, and for those who, in buying his ability to do this work, were entitled to and did appropriate to themselves the chief credit for having done it."

DeGroot had several other publications credited to him, including an article in *U.S. Mineral Resources, 1866,* his "Report on the Mineral Deposits and Other Properties of the Nevada Consolidated Borax Company" (San Francisco, 1871), "The Comstock Lode," an 1873 article for the *Overland Monthly,* and an 1884

pamphlet, *Recollections of California Mining Life.*
Birge referred to DeGroot as having an unusual
character which combined an ambition to lift himself
into better conditions with an indifference to personal
comforts: "Though the Doctor rarely had any money,
except what was loose in the outside pocket of an old
gray coat, what he had was generously given to any old
friend that appealed to his sympathies. Not six months
ago I paid the Doctor a small sum of money, and
suggested to him the policy of applying it wholly to his
own use. While we talked, an old acquaintance 'struck'
him for aid and was refused. I believe the Doctor saw
the amusement I felt at his poor affectation of severity,
for with a quick glance at my face and without a word
to me he turned, and running after his friend, divided
with him. He had less than five dollars to divide.
Returning to me he said decisively, 'You think I'm a
fool; I've known that man thirty years; he's been a hard
worker, and there ought to be some way of providing
for such men without sending them to the almshouse.'
He was of quick perception, sympathetic, always ready
with information and labor to help his friends, and
never spoke a harsh word of any one, however much
imposed upon."

DeGroot, according to Birge, was a man of exemplary
character: "His speech always absolutely free from
profanity or vulgarity; he made no use of tobacco in any
form, and though he believed liquor much less harmful
than tobacco, he always declared that his necessities
were all the stimulant he required."

He was a hardy man who worked hard and exercised
all his life. DeGroot did this at his pleasure, however,
for Birge wrote of him: "The Doctor was of a highly
sensitive, nervous temperament, and could not submit
to such restraint as fixed hours for work."

DeGroot also possessed nerve and physical stamina,
as his friend related: "He did not know what fear of
physical harm was. This absence of fear grew out of
exposures to danger and escapes unharmed, until it
would seem that a confidence in an unseen power that
protected him was justified. That he had full belief that

no harm would come to him is a fact. I well remember an incident in a rough mining camp, where the only public room in the 'hotel' was a bar room, and about as rough an assemblage got together there as could be found anywhere. One of these was a burly fellow, evidently desirous of establishing himself as a terror, and not quite drunk enough knowingly to risk any danger of tackling the wrong man. DeGroot came in from a hard day's work, looking unusually small and inoffensive without a coat or vest, and was immediately spotted by the bully as a likely butt for vulgar wit. He was evidently surprised and angered by the good-natured, quick, and fearless repartee of the Doctor, and with an oath rushed on him fiercely. Before I could interfere, quicker than I can tell it, just a revolving mass of old clothes and heels, and our terror was on his back, pinned down by the Doctor as by a clothespin. The fight was over. The bully retired, and the bar was liberally patronized in honor of the little 'old man,' who was probably the least excited of any one in the room.''

Henry DeGroot was killed in 1893 when he was struck by a passing locomotive while standing near the railroad tracks. He was about seventy-eight years old.

I

Discovery and Early History of the Great Washoe Lode— Singular Misapprehensions in Regard to the Facts.

That the Comstock lode, in the item of active production, surpasses every other gold and silver bearing ore channel of which we have any knowledge, admits of no question. Other veins may have been discovered and worked in both South America and Mexico, carrying ores of higher grade, and from which larger aggregate sums may in the course of centuries have been taken, but from none of them has the annual product of bullion been half or perhaps one-quarter so great as from this. These slow going countries, with their crude machinery and their man and mule power, required 10 years to accomplish what we, with the aid of steam and other modern inventions, accomplish in one. Throughout all the mining regions of Spanish America it was formerly, as it is almost everywhere still the custom, to bring the ore to the surface on the backs of men, to raise the water in buckets and drive the arastras and nearly all other machinery by mule power, as many as 1,400 of these animals having been kept for this purpose and for treading the patios, in the district of Guanajuato alone. The machinery employed on some half-dozen claims on the Comstock lode would be more than sufficient to perform the service exacted from these 1,400 overworked and underfed brutes, supplemented by whole armies of equally hard-faring men. It is this capacity to

Perform Much in a Short Time

that gives to the mother lode of Washoe its superior importance as compared with the most renowned *Veta Madre* of these older and historically famous mining countries. And yet the out-turn of these latter has for more than 300 years been remarked upon by scientists and political economists as of vital consequence to the commerce and industries of the world. The chroniclers of the past notice it as a feat worthy of special comment that Mexico and South America combined should have been able to turn out gold and silver at the rate of $20,000,000 per year. Since the conquest of Mexico by the Spaniards, that country has produced an annual average of only about $8,000,000, this being the rate at which Peru and Bolivia, the great bullion producing countries of South America, have turned out the precious metals in the meantime.

The State of Nevada has yielded to date over $300,000,000, being at the rate of $20,000,000 per year since the business of mining was here first actively engaged in. Of this total about two-thirds came from the several mines situated on the Comstock range. The most prolific ledge in Mexico yielded during a period of 284 years an average of not quite $2,500,000 per annum, while the richest in South America, that of Cerro del Potosi, in Bolivia, yielded less than $5,000,000 per annum during the 250 years it was worked.

From two claims on the Comstock, the Crown Point and the Belcher, covering jointly a lineal section of 1,480 feet of the ledge, there were extracted, in the space of three years, $50,000,000, of which one-half was disbursed in dividends to the shareholders. Within the past two years there have been taken from the Consolidated Virginia mine alone about $35,000,000, of which over $20,000,000 were net profits. During the year 1873 the dividends declared to shareholders in the various mines along the Comstock amounted to $22,000,000, a rate of clear earnings that has since been maintained.

That the Productive Era

of an ore channel so vast and marked by features of such permanence will extend into the distant future may well be expected, this being in accordance with geological facts and all previous experience. History teaches that silver mines situated at these high altitudes and occupying great natural chasms never wholly give out. Mexican mines opened by the Aztecs still continue to yield well, and there are districts in Spain that were operated before the Christian era, which to this day richly repay the labor bestowed upon them. In many parts of Europe there are silver mines now being worked with profit that were opened from 500 to 1,000 years ago, though none of them exhibit the masterly proportions of the great dominating lode of Nevada.

That the facts connected with

The Discovery and Early History

of a gold and silver bearing vein that has already yielded so largely of the previous metals, and is destined to occupy such a conspicuous place in the annals of mining, should have been so misapprehended, not to say strangely perverted, is a circumstance to be accounted for only on the hypotheses of sheer carelessness or indifference on the part of those who first undertook to make public record of this event. According to the generally received version of this affair, the finding of the Comstock lode was due to certain parties who, while excavating a hole to collect water for gold washing, threw up a quantity of earth mixed with free gold and the decomposed sulphurets of silver, this rich material consisting of the disintegrated outcrop of the main lode which here came to the surface. This excavation was made on the dividing line between the old Mexican and Ophir claims, being near the southerly end of the present Ophir ground. Prior to this incident, which occurred in the latter part of May or early in June, 1859, James Finney, commonly known as

3

"Old Virginny," had located a quartz claim on the line of croppings a little to the west of the Comstock, afterwards known as the Virginia ledge, but had done no work upon it. This claim, which was recorded on the 22nd day of February, 1858, was taken up because the locator considered it to be on the ledge previously occupied and already extensively worked at Gold Hill, a mile and a quarter further south. These croppings, though quite bold, were not, however, on that ledge at all, or at least not on the main Comstock, which as has since been shown, lies several hundred feet to the east of them.

The Real Site of the First Discovery.

Now, it will not be denied that the ground of Consolidated Imperial Company is on and constitutes a section of the Comstock lode, and as this ground was occupied and extensively worked as early as 1857, it follows that the discovery of the lode must antedate that event. More than a year before Finney had taken up his claim on the croppings of the Virginia ledge and more than two years before Peter O'Reilly and Patrick McLaughlin, the gold washers, had dug the excavation mentioned, a number of arastras were being run on the rich ores at Gold Hill, quite a hamlet having already sprung up at that place. That the parties operating here had little idea of the magnitude or importance of the lode they were working and were wholly ignorant of its extension either to the north or south must be admitted. But that they were really on the Comstock and were well advised as to its character at that particular point, cannot be questioned. If to any one, then, the credit of discovering this lode is due, it belongs to these quartz workers at Gold Hill, who had been opening it up and crushing its ores for so long a time before the rich surface deposits were struck upon it farther north at Virginia City. It is not claimed that there was much merit in their being there. They had worked out Gold canyon, which afforded fair placer diggings, and having arrived at its head and found there a heavy reef of rich quartz, went to work upon it, treating it simply as an auriferous ore, never dreaming that it would at greater depths run into silver, or that heavy deposits of that metal existed in the neighborhood.

The Grosch Brothers.

So far as searching after argentiferous ores was concerned, the idea does not appear to have entered the heads of any of these pioneer Washoe miners, if we except from the number H.B. and E.A. Grosch, commonly spoken of as the Grosch Brothers, two young men who came over to this region from Placerville, California, in 1852. While they made gold washing their principal business, they seem to have entertained the idea that there was silver also in the country, and being educated mineralogists, with some knowledge of metallurgy, spent much time in seeking after this class of ores. That they succeeded in finding what they considered silver-bearing lodes is well established, they having carried to California and there exhibited samples of ore carrying a considerable percentage of that metal. By some it has been claimed that they obtained these samples from the Comstock ledge. But this is obviously a mistake, unless we consider the ore channel that passes through the present Dayton claim as being on the mother lode, for there can be no question but they obtained their best specimens from that neighborhood. On a sort of bench, 200 feet above the American ravine, and on a line with the Dayton croppings, the remains of a shaft sunk by these young men are still to be seen, the fragments of a rude furnace erected near by and used by them in experimenting upon their ores being also visible in 1859. They probably never pushed their researches further north than Gold Hill. Certain it is, if they had ever found any of the rich silver ores of the Comstock proper, or at least such as were first struck at Virginia City, they, being qualified to appreciate their value, would have taken measures to secure the discovery and turn it to practical account. The fact is, they never found any ores of that character; yet to these

5

men more than to any others is due the merit of having first paid attention to the subject, and of actually engaging in a search after silver ores on the "Eastern slope;" and it is not improbably that they would, had their lives been spared a little longer, have been instrumental in making more important discoveries of this metal.

Next to these brothers in the list of those who may with any propriety claim even an indirect agency in bringing about the discovery of the great Washoe *Veta Madre,* stand the early Gold Hill quartz miners, followed by Finney, O'Reilly and McLaughlin in the order mentioned, Comstock, whose name the lode bears having had no more to do with that event than the man who is supposed to occupy the lunar attendant on our planet. The circumstances that led to this singular and awkward misnomer will be explained in the next number of the Comstock Papers.

II

First Strike of the "Black Stuff"— Conflicting Claims and their Adjustment— How the Great Washoe Lode Came to be Named.

As already related, the discovery of the Comstock lode at a new point near the present site of Virginia City, was occasioned by a couple of gold washers' digging a shallow pit to hold water for the use of their rockers. This event, which occurred in the month of June, 1859, was the result of the sheerest accident. These men were not hunting for silver nor ores of any kind. In so far as they had any idea about such substances, this was the thing they were most desirous of avoiding. While working up Six Mile canyon the year before, they and their companions, as they approached its head, had encountered a dark colored, heavy metallic rock, "black stuff" as they called it, which had caused them no little trouble, its weight being so nearly that of the gold obtained along the canyon that they found it difficult to separate the two in their rockers. All the gold dust gathered in that region of country, containing a large percentage of silver, was much lighter than the average California dust, and consequently more difficult to save by the process of washing. When, therefore, these honest miners detected in the pit they had sunk the presence of this detestable stuff — the rich sulphurets of silver, they were disgusted thereat, and would have heaved it aside and paid no further attention to it had they not found mixed up with the earth thrown out a considerable amount of free gold. This was an article with which they were acquainted — was, in fact, the thing they

7

were searching for, wherefore they at once proceeded to take up a surface or placer claim at that point.

A Multiplicity of Claimants to the New Discovery.

Now, so it was, this precise spot happened to be within the boundaries of the ground located by Finney the year before, or this, at least, was the view the old man chose to take of the matter, and not, perhaps, without some show of reason, as it was then the custom of the district to make square locations in taking up both quartz and placer claims, and it might well have been that his claim the croppings on which lay only a few rods further west, included this spot within its limits. Joseph Kirby, who had previously been washing along a small ravine a little below this place, also advanced some sort of claim to an interest in the new discovery, there being several others who, upon one pretext or another, were seeking a share in it.

Affairs being thus complicated,

Henry P. Comstock,

an old resident and common friend of all the contestants, was elected, or perhaps elected himself, to act as umpire in the premises; an office he seems to have performed to his own satisfaction, and for aught that appears to the contrary, to the satisfaction of all concerned. In adjusting the business it was so arranged that the umpire appeared on the record as the owner of most of the property in dispute, he having first awarded it to Finney, and then bought the latter out. The claim in question covered what are now known as the Bonanza mines, and also a part of the present Ophir ground. Within a year from the time the above transaction took place, it sold for a million of dollars. That the other parties to his contest should have so readily yielded their pretensions and acquiesced in the disposition thus made of the property is explained by the fact that they did not consider it of any special value, and had not, probably, much confidence themselves in either the justice or validity of their claims.

He Receives for his Mine an Indian Pony and Something to Drink Beside.

The consideration that moved the vendor to make over his estate in this mining claim consisted of a certain Indian pony, bobtailed, lean and aged, of which the purchaser was then and there possessed, this constituting the sum total of his available effects, save only a scanty supply of cabin traps, a roll of blankets, a gold rocker and a rifle, with a reasonable stock of whisky and tobacco, without which latter, existence with these early dwellers on the "Eastern slope" would have been intolerable, if not wholly impracticable.

While Finney did not guarantee title to the ground sold, the transfer thereof having been effected by simple quit claim deed, he did, on the other hand, require that his friend should in the bill of sale assure title to the animal made over to him, the abbreviated caudal appendage of the brute and some other marks about him pointing to a former ownership by the Piutes, against any claim from which quarter the old man was naturally desirous of protecting himself. According to some authorities, divers bottles of exhilarating fluids formed part of the consideration by Finney received on that occasion; a fact which no one having any acquaintance with the convivial habits and commercial usages of these Washoe pioneers will feel inclined to call in question. Indeed, that class of persons may be said to inferentially know that such was the case, a drink all 'round having been with these pioneers not only a pledge of friendship but a token with which they sealed all bargains.

He Sells His Claim to a California "Rock Sharp."

Very soon after he had acquired his claim, Comstock disposed of the greater portion of it to Judge Walsh, an enterprising and experienced quartz miner of Grass Valley, who, having heard of this discovery and seen some of the rich ore brought to his place, hastened over the mountains for the purpose of examining the deposit and making a purchase thereof, if the thing looked favorable. How little appreciation Comstock himself had of the real value of this property is evinced by the fact that he parted with his interest in nearly the whole of it for $6,000, congratulating himself that he had been able to dispose of it for even that much, and joining with his associates in making merry over the manner in which he had taken in what they facetiously termed, "the California rock sharp."

How His Name Came to be Conferred on the Lode.

In making out the deed whereby this claim was conveyed to Walsh, it was, for the want of a better name, described as the "Comstock ground," a style of description which, having been adhered to in all subsequent sales of the property or portions thereof, caused this term to be at length applied to all portions of the lode. Other than this there was no especial fitness in thus designating the great ore channel, the man whose name it bears having had nothing to do with its discovery, location or subsequent development, and who acquired all the interest he ever had in it at a very cheap rate.

III

An Error Corrected — First Samples of Ore that reached California.

We find, on conversing with certain of the early Washoe miners, that we erred in the last number of these papers, in saying that Comstock owned the most of the rich ground purchased by Judge Walsh, and that the property so bought was described as the Comstock claim in the deed of transfer made on that occasion. The facts connected with his first visit to Washoe, his return and subsequent purchases, as we have them from Judge Walsh himself, were these: Towards the latter part of June, 1859, B.A. Harrison, then keeping cattle on Truckee meadows, brought some pieces of the rich Comstock ore over the mountains to Grass Valley, where the Judge was engaged in quartz mining. This ore had been given to Harrison while on his way to California by a man named Stone, with directions to take it over to Grass Valley and have it tested, its weight leading him to believe that it contained a good deal of metal of some kind or another. Stone, who resided at Stone & Gates' crossing, a well known locality on Truckee river, had been to the mines and there obtained this ore, and having a notion like many others, that it might be valuable, availed himself of the first opportunity that offered for having its character determined.

The Assay and its Results.

Judge Walsh, to whom Harrison had given these samples on his arrival at Grass Valley, took them to Melville Atwood, who was then carrying on the business of assayer at that place, and instructed him to

11

make an assay of them, being himself satisfied that the ore was rich in the precious metals. Mr. Atwood made two assays from the same piece of ore and found it to contain $3,000 in silver and $876 in gold — a total of $3,876 to the ton. These assays, undoubtedly the first ever had of the Comstock ore, were made on the 27th day of June, 1859. The two buttons obtained and the pieces of ore from which the assay samples were taken, handsomely mounted and inclosed under glass, are to be seen in the office of Almarin B. Paul, of this city, with the certificates of Atwood and Harrison, attesting their genuineness appended thereto. There was residing in Grass Valley at this time Richard Killala, an accomplished Irish metallurgist, also several German assayers, all of whom were well acquainted with this class of ores, and readily divined the importance of the discovery, having had more or less experience in silver mining countries.

The Ophir Ground — How it was Held and the Prices obtained for it.

Encouraged by the opinions of these men and taking council of his own judgment, Walsh at once set out for Washoe, the name by which the region of the country where this deposit had been found then first began to be known. Arriving at the spot early in July, the Judge remained there a week or more during which time he became so well convinced that this ore-find was likely to prove valuable that he determined to buy out some of the parties laying claim to it. In pursuance of this purpose he came home, supplied himself with money and at once returned, reaching the mines toward the latter part of July. By this time a number of locations had been made along the supposed line of the main lode, to which latter there had as yet been given no name. The principal of these claims consisted of the Ophir, embracing 1,500 feet, with the Central 150 feet; the California 300 feet, and the Central No. 2, 100 feet, adjoining it in the order mentioned on the south.

Finney's claim to the rich spot on the Ophir ground

having been gotten rid of in the manner already narrated, that location was now owned by the following parties: (100 feet, afterwards known as the Mexican ground, having previously been disposed of.) Henry P. Comstock, Joseph Winters, one twenty-fourth; Houseworth, one twenty-fourth and Oburn one-twelfth. Judge Walsh bought Penrod's one-sixth, paying him $6,200 therefor; also Comstock's one-sixth paying him about the same amount, besides $5,000 for one-third of the California ground, and some small and unimportant locations he had made further south. In the early part of August, Morrison and Hearst bought out McLaughlin for $2,500. Later in the fall John O. Earl and Judge Walsh purchased O'Reilly's interest paying $36,000 therefor, the Winters having retained their interest for a considerable length of time. In all the purchases and sales made by Judge Walsh, as well as in the other operations carried on by him in Washoe, Joseph Woodworth was his equal partner.

The Mexican Claim.

As stated above, 100 feet of the original Ophir ground had been disposed of before the sales here mentioned were effected. This section, commencing 200 feet from the south end of the claim and embracing the richest portion of it, had been given by the joint owners thereof to Penrod, Osburn, and Comstock, as a consideration for two cheap arrastras that they had put up for the use and benefit of the company. Penrod, who owned one-half of this section, sold the same in October to the Maldonado brothers, for $3,000, the other half having been sold to Osburn and Comstock to Hughes and others for about the same sum. The Maldonado's being of Spanish origin led to this piece of ground being called first the Spanish and afterwards the Mexican claim. In the early part of 1861 the Maldonado's sold this ground to the houses of Alsop & Co., and Duncan, Sherman & Co., for $200,000. These parties failing to manage the property with much energy or good judgment, tired of the ownership and afterwards disposed of it to the Ophir company for $30,000. It now forms a part of the present Ophir mine.

First Arrival of Ore in San Francisco — Heavy Costs and Big Returns.

Early in the month of September, Judge Walsh came to San Francisco bringing with him 3,150 pounds of selected ore taken from the first opening made on the Ophir ground. This ore was worked by Mosheimer & Kustel, and netted him $4,871. The cost of transportation, there having been as yet no wagon roads built over the mountains, was, as a matter of course, very great. Later in this month, Walsh and his associates in the mine commenced the regular shipment of ore to the city, having by the first of November, when the snow rendered the mountains difficult of passage by wagons, sent down 38 tons, which, worked by the same parties, gave a gross yield of $114,000 exactly $3,000 per ton. The cost of freight and reduction on this lot was at the rate of $512 per ton.

The Washoe Excitement Begins.

This bullion, which was placed on exhibition in the banking house of Alsop & Co., first began to arouse the moneyed classes to the importance of this new discovery, and infect the popular mind with the idea of silver mining. A good many miners with some speculators, traders and adventurers in general, had already made their way over the Sierra Nevada, there having been gathered in the Washoe region a thousand or more of this class before the winter set in. The newspapers also, for several month's before had teemed with favorable accounts of the mines over there. But these had been generally regarded as exaggerated or over colored statements, such as usually emanate from excited and interested parties, and had therefore produced no very marked influence upon either capitalists, speculators or the working masses. The sight of this ore and the resultant bullion had the effect, however, to awaken up everybody, and before the

14

winter was half over, thousands were making preparations to emigrate to the new land of promise.

Different Views Held by Different Parties

Meantime, not a few who had secured interests in the new mines, being timid or acting under the advice of those presumed to be safe counselors, hastened to dispose of the same, realizing often very inadequate prices. Among others accorded a high reputation for scientific knowledge and claiming a practical acquaintance with silver mining, but who still entertained a very poor opinion of this Washoe discovery, was the French engineer of mines, M. Lauer, sent out by his government to examine and report upon the gold mines of California. So little faith had he in this discovery that he advised his friends to part with their interests as soon as they could realize the smallest profits, his course in this respect having been practically endorsed by some of our resident experts who had enjoyed a long experience at silver mining in South America and in different parts of Mexico.

Among those who had visited and examined the deposits in the new district, few shared in the opinion held by these more learned men; and it is but just to say the early Washoe miners, notwithstanding they were so ready to sell out, professed the greatest confidence in the richness and permanency of the mines themselves; this seeming inconsistency being explained by the fact that they were all very poor, and wished to make a small stake at the first opportunity; every one of them believing, moreover, that he would be able, as soon as he had sold these first claims, to go and find others equally valuable. Messrs. Woodworth and Walsh relate, that while camping with Comstock, near the claim purchased of him, he pointed to the spot where Virginia City now stands, and declared his conviction that it would soon become the site of a great city, and that the mine he was about to sell them would yet turn out to be one of the biggest in the world. It is true, such ex-

15

pressions as these might be attributed to that spirit of gasconade in which Comstock was so apt to indulge, and through the exercise of which he afterwards succeeded in having his name applied to the whole of this Washoe lode; yet the prediction seemed, under the circumstances, so improbable that one regarding it as somewhat prophetic, feels inclined to credit these utterances as having been made with a degree of sincerity at least.

IV

Mineral Wealth of Western Utah— Early Traditions and Opinions on the Subject— First Silver Ore Found in '49.

It is an error to suppose that the discovery of silver mines east of the Sierra Nevada was to the people of California wholly a surprise. Antecedent to that event, many people in this State had, for various reasons entertained the idea that deposits of this metal existed in the expanse of country laid down on the early maps as the Great American desert, and latterly known as the Utah basin. First, the region lay contiguous to, and following the trend of the great mountain chains, directly in the path of the silver producing belts of Mexico. Then there were Spanish legends ascribing to it a great wealth of this kind, stories of successful expeditions thither in search of the precious metals having come down to us from former times. Many intelligent persons, more especially those conversant with Mexican history, cherished the belief that important discoveries would some day be made off that way. Among this number was Judge James M. Crane, an early settler in California, but who, impressed with this opinion, passed over the mountains in 1857, and took up his abode at Genoa, then the principal town in Western Utah, to represent which section he was afterwards chosen delegate to Congress. Crane, who had made himself familiar with the mining chronicles of Northern Mexico, was an enthusiast on the subject, and after traveling much over Western Utah, now the State of Nevada, predicted that it would soon become conspicuous for its production of the precious metals, and even outrank California in this respect. As this was before the discovery of the Comstock lode, the expression of this opinion may be supposed to have been due to some mental prevision of these after events. What was then foretold has already come to pass; the gray deserts of Nevada produce to-day more than twice as much bullion as the "Golden State."

The venerable pioneer and eminently good man,

Peter Lassen,

when crossing the Black Rock country, in northwestern Nevada, observed there such signs of silver bearing lodes as induced him to return in 1858 and prospect that region, and but for his untimely death at the hands of Indians, while out on that expedition, it is probably enough that he would have attained the object of his search.

Nor was the existence of the precious metal in these desert lands to the east a mere matter of opinion or conjecture founded on traditions and theories alone. The survivors of the immigrant party, so many of whom perished in Death valley in the fall of 1849, while making their way over the mountains into California found and brought with them some pieces of very rich silver ore. So rich, in fact, was this ore that it attracted the attention of all whom saw it and led to many parties going afterwards to search for the place where it was found. Associating the locality with the scene of these immigrants' sufferings the most of these parties sought for it in the vicinity of Death valley, going, as recent experience had shown, much too far east. Last year some miners prospecting in the Coso mountains, Inyo County, came upon the exact spot where this ore was obtained, its identity being established by the most ample and unmistakable proofs. It is situated in what is now known as the Lee district, the ledges from which this rich ore was broken off being at present owned by the Emigrant company, who are working them with capital results. The finding of this rich ore by these immigrants ante-dates the discovery of the Comstock lode nearly ten years during all which time the attention of prospectors and explorers was more or less occupied with the subject of mineral discoveries off in that direction.

Brewing of the Washoe Excitement.

With the public mind thus somewhat prepared for an event of the kind, it is not at all strange that a large number of Californians were ready to credit the report and to take their departure for the "Eastern Slope," the name by which this trans-Alpine region had come to be known immediately upon the announcement being made of this rich metaliferous find over there. Only the year before many thousand miners had precipitately left the State for British Columbia, but meeting with only disappointment there, the greater portion of them had already returned to their old haunts. Once on the wing, however, the most of these men remained uneasy and ready for a new flight should anything occur to set them in motion. Being in this condition of industrial disorder and mental unrest, the discovery of these silver mines opened to this class a new and inviting El Dorado, the evidences of whose wealth rested not, as in the case of Frasier river, upon dubious rumors and the statements of interested parties, but on the more substantial proof of ore shipments and bars of bullion.

As already stated, Judge Walsh had before the end of 1859 brought to San Francisco, ore that yielded nearly $120,000 worth of gold and silver. In addition to this other parties had shipped to the city some small lots of rich ore and as there had been a considerable number of arrastras kept running at the mines, with some gold dust gathered from the placers, the total bullion product of these Washoe mines for the year must have exceeded $200,000; the whole of it produced with a comparatively small outlay of labor, and in the course of about six month's working time. There was no gainsaying this sort of evidence. Here were ocular and tangible proofs such as any reasonable mind would accept as conclusively establishing the great value of the mines. Such, at least was the view that the masses were

19

pleased to take of this matter, and by the time that winter had set in these facts, growing as they spread, had become widely disseminated throughout the State, creating a great excitement among all classes, and inspiring multitudes everywhere with the purpose of an early emigration to a region that promised an easily gained fortune to all, and the opening up to capital and enterprise of a new and profitable industry. Already, then, by the end of the year there had been laid the foundation for a mining stampede of more formidable proportions than any that had preceded it, the movement having been partially restrained for two or three months until the snow had settled on the Sierra Nevada, these mountains, before the construction of wagon roads over them, having been difficult of passage during the winter.

Meantime, the adventurers who had already gathered on the

"Eastern Slope"

had not been idle. Before the winter set in, though it commenced that year with much rigor, on the 2nd of November, these wide-awake and active men had taken up every thing in the shape of quartz croppings along and adjacent to the line of the main lode. The surrounding country for a distance of fifty miles or more had been prospected and many new mining districts laid out, in each one of which a great many company claims had been located and upon some of the latter much work had been done. Foreseeing the urgent necessity that would soon arise for the employment of propulsive power the waters of the Carson river, had for many miles been claimed for this purpose. All the more available creeks, springs, wood and farming lands had been taken up, the latter having in many instances been surveyed and partially secured by enclosure or other improvements. Some water driven arrastras had been put up along the Carson, and steps taken for the construction of more extensive and efficient reduction works, at the mines. Virginia City had been laid out and several substantial stone buildings, with a much larger number of wood, canvas or other temporary structures, erected on the spot. The hamlet at Gold Hill had doubled its size, while Carson City, which the summer before had drawn to it most of the business from the old Mormon town of Genoa, had grown from some half dozen housed into a good sized village. Numerous town sites had been selected at other supposed eligible points, upon all of which cities of magnificent proportions had been projected. Notwithstanding the difficulties and great cost of transportation over the mountains several traders were able to show very respectable stocks of goods, and not had the following winter proved to be one of unusual severity, there would have been provisions enough in the country to have subsisted the population until spring with comfort. As it was, many were forced to forego the use of most of their accustomed luxuries at the table, not few having been content before the winter was over to accept for rations a short allowance of beans and bacon.

It might prove interesting to the public of to-day to say something here of the history of this Washoe country, prior to the period of which we are now speaking, when it was as yet occupied by an almost evenly divided population of Mormons or Gentiles, whose religious and social differences lead to animosities that made these remote secluded valleys the scenes of perpetual turmoil and strife, converting them not unfrequently into the theatres of fearful tragedies and revolting crimes, and we should feel inclined to devote a chapter to the narration of these strange and little known events, did not this involve such a wide departure from the original purpose of these papers as to forbid the undertaking.

V

A Hard Winter and its Results.

The winter of 1859 commenced early, as much as a foot of snow having fallen at Virginia City on the 2d of November; and, although this storm was succeeded by several weeks of pleasant weather, the winter that followed was a severe one. As yet not more than a dozen comfortable houses had been put up at Virginia City and Gold Hill; wherefore the several hundred adventurers who had gathered at the mines were compelled to live and lodge in tents, canvas houses, mud and stone built huts and such other temporary abodes as could be constructed from the rude and scanty material at hand, there being very little timber to be had. Some, whose means were not very abundant, burrowed Indian fashion in dirt-covered holes dug in the ground, while a few even found shelter in the mouths of the tunnels that had been started for opening up the mines. The public lodging houses were well patronized institutions, every inch of space, even to the floors, having been utilized for sleeping purposes. In these places rows of bunks, reaching from floors to ceiling, one above the other, ran around the sides, with a double tier extending through the center of the building, each of these shelf-like bunks being furnished with a coarse hay mattress and a limited supply of woolen blankets. Of nights, chairs, tables and counters were made to do service as bedsteads. For this sort of accommodation one dollar per night was exacted, lodgers being charged half price for the privilege of spreading their blankets on the floor.

Huddled into these miserable dormitories, the weather much of the time stormy and intensely cold, a good deal of suffering was experienced before the winter was over; nor were the unhappy lodgers permitted always to enjoy even this sort of shelter without interruption and disturbance. Frequently the gales that came tearing down the sides of Mount Davidson would, in the middle of the night, when all were wrapt in sweet slumber, dreaming of rich croppings, black sulphurets and wire silver, rend to tatters their canvass dormitory, or taking it up bodily turn the thing inside out, leaving the hapless sleepers exposed to the peltings of the pitiless storm. To aptly describe the scenes that attended the sudden uncovering of these embryotic silver miners, howling and swearing as they sought to screen their half-naked persons under the fluttering fragments of their disruptured tabernacle or hastened off through the storm in search of shelter elsewhere, would require the pen of a Dickens.

A Hopeful Crowd and a Winter Emigration. — High Prices of Provisions and Provender.

But not withstanding their miserable situation few of these sojourners in the new El Dorado grew disheartened or sought greater comforts by a return to California. On the contrary, such was their confidence in the mineral wealth of the country, that they resolved to hold out at all hazards till spring, when they believed they would be able, on the disappearance of the snow and the advent of good weather, to verify all that had been said of the richness of the mines and realize their fondest expectations. The high hopes entertained by those already over the mountains had the effect to so stimulate the excitement in California that quite an emigration was kept up throughout the winter, the population collected at the new mines having amounted by the end of April to about 2,000.

By this time the condition of things had become decidedly rough. The winter had proved to be one of unusual length and severity. The early settlers in Carson Valley, a shiftless people at best, not having expected such a large influx of population nor anticipated so hard a winter, had failed to provide for these contingencies by gathering more hay and raising more farm produce than usual. Having their attention absorbed by mining matters they had, in fact, made hardly as great provision of this kind as in ordinary years. The consequence was, there soon began to be a dearth of these commodities, the prices advancing to enormous rates before spring. Hay, for example, sold at the rate of four and five and barley at six and eight hundred dollars per ton, provisions of all kinds being also excessively scarce and dear. Many of the horses and two-thirds of the cattle in the country died from starvation. The simplest fare, such as hardly more than sufficed to keep life in his body, cost the miner three-fold more than the most luxurious living would so in California. Believing, however, that relief would come with the spring, all bore these burdens and deprivations bravely. Knowing that supplies of all kinds would be rushed in from California as soon as the mountains became passable to pack trains, there was little murmuring or complaint.

Things Get a Set-Back— An Indian War Foolishly Begun and Disastrously Ended.

While all were thus hopeful and patient and were even in the best of spirits, there occured one of those foolish but fatal events which, through the want of a little forethought and practical sense on the parts of the multitude, result often in disaster alike to individuals and the community at large. There were living on Carson river, 20 miles below Virginia City, three brothers named Williams, who there kept a sort of public house, their reputation for square dealing being none of the best. Among other evil practices imputed to these men was that of cheating the Indians and grossly abusing their squaws, in which account the Pah Utes cherished towards them a deadly animosity, awaiting only a favorable opportunity to be avenged upon them. Accordingly, one night, early in the month of May, 1860, a small band of savages attacked the house of

25

these brothers and slew the occupants, four in number. It so happened that three of these were strangers, merely stopping there over night, only one of the Williamses having been amongst the slain. However much the brothers themselves might have deserved the fate that had overtaken one of their number, this butchery of innocent parties was not to be overlooked, nor would it do to allow the savages to redress their wrongs, fancied or real, in this summary way, anyhow. As soon, therefore, as

The News of the Massacre

reached the settlements, it was determined that the guilty parties should be sought out and punished. As the Indians, before leaving, had set fire to and burnt up the house and all that was in it, the names of the strangers killed were never ascertained, they probably having been miners prospecting in the neighborhood. It was well known that only a small number of Indians had been engaged in the killing and that the head men and great mass of these people know nothing about it. Wherefore the older settlers in the valley advised that a few of their own number should visit the principle camps of the Pah Utes, and consult with the chiefs about the affair, offering a reward for the apprehension and surrender to the whites of the guilty parties and threatening the whole of them with punishment if the offenders were not found and given up. Had this course been adopted the criminals no doubt would at little expense and trouble have soon been secured and properly dealt with. But there had by this time collected in the new mining region a good many young men, brave and chivalrous but impulsive and inconsiderate, who were not inclined to pursue this wise and considerate course, believing and advocating that an armed force should at once be fitted out and sent to inflict upon the savages instant, severe and indiscriminate punishment. Endorsing this view were a few men of a different stripe — men of ruffian proclivities, who, believing that an Indian war would furnish them employment at the public expense, and possibly afford opportunities for securing Pah Ute ponies at a cheap rate, did all that lay in their power to promote a scrimmage of this kind.

The Avengers Go for the Savages but Meet With a Repulse.

The party of violence being thus in the ascendant, a company of something over a hundred men was raised, armed and mounted, and, under the command of Major Ormsby, of Carson City, started down the Truckee river intending to first clean out the Indian rancheria situated on the border of Pyramid lake, at the mouth of that stream. The Indians, however, having got wind of their purpose, entrenched themselves behind the rocks on either side of a narrow gorge along the river through which their foes had to pass. The whites, ignorant of their presence, marched into this defile and when half-way through it were fired upon so suddenly that they were thrown into confusion and obliged to retreat precipitately, not being able to make any effected resistance. The Indians making pursuit killed some ten or fifteen of their enemies, wounding as many more, Major Ormsby having been amongst the slain. Only after they had drawn them from their covert did the whites succeed in killing any of the Indians, the number of the fallen having been about equal on both sides.

A Big Scare and a Bad Business Altogether.

When the discomfited survivors reached Virginia City, great was the excitement that at once ensued, it being generally supposed that the savages, emboldened by their success, would instantly march upon that place in overwhelming numbers. Consternation everywhere prevailed. Nothing was thought of but defense against the approaching foe, whose movements were watched by scouts sent out for the purpose. The approaches to the city were guarded and sentinels stationed on the hills around. The women and children were gathered into places of safety, the most of them having been corralled in a large half-finished stone house put up by Peter O'Reilly, which was then strongly barricaded. Couriers were dispatched to California, advising the people and authorities there of the critical situation and imploring them for aid; arms, troops, ammunition, grub and whisky having been hurried over the mountains in response to this call. Arriving, these auxiliary forces joined the veterans already in the field, and soon between three and four hundred men, well equipped and officered by Jack Hayes and other experienced Indian fighters, were on their way to give battle to the dread Pah Utes, every man of them fairly bloated with valor and a fixed determination to exterminate the hated race, leaving not so much as a papoose or a mehela behind. But the hated race had got well out of the way, having run off into the northern deserts, where the whites, finding they could not reach, decided not to pursue them. The Indians had, in fact, retreated north immediately after the fight on the Truckee, having been running in one direction while the whites were running another. Nobody was therefore killed on either side during this second expedition, which returned to the abodes of civilization and the pursuits of peace without scalps or glory.

This scare, which had, as we have seen, so little foundation in fact, proved a serious detriment to all the leading interests of Washoe. To say nothing of the heavy public debt attending it, the country was set back fully a year through the alarm created and the check put upon enterprise and the influx of capital and population. Had the writer consulted his feelings alone he would have ignored the story of this miserable business altogether; but a sense of duty has constrained him to allude to it thus briefly, that a lesson so instructive might not be wholly lost to the future.

VI

The Pioneer Locators on the Comstock — Their Fate and Their Fortunes.

As some account of the history and subsequent fortunes of the men who first located claims on the Comstock lode, or who, through the purchase of interests, the construction of mills or otherwise, became prominently identified with its early annals, might prove of interest to the general reader, we will at this stage of our remarks and before proceeding to speak of the era of its active development, give to the public such scraps of information on these points as we can now recall to mind or have been able to pick up from conversations with Washoe pioneers. It may be observed at the outset, that a large proportion of these men, once seemingly so favored of fortune or who enjoyed such rare opportunities for the easy acquisition of wealth, are now dead, only moderately rich, or abjectly poor. Although but little more than seventeen years have elapsed since the occurrence of these events, more than half the fist locators on the Comstock lode are dead, while very few of the survivors are possessed of large pecuniary means; results attributable, in good degree, to their liberal and improvident habits, coupled very often with a rough and careless life.

Comstock Himself

soon spent the proceeds realized from the sale of his different pieces of mining ground, amounting, perhaps, to twelve or fifteen thousand dollars altogether. After remaining about Virginia City for five or six years, during which he made many prospecting tours into the country adjacent, he left his old stamping grounds and went to Montana, where he perished from a pistol shot through the head inflicted by his own hand while laboring under temporary insanity. This condition of mind was induced by hardships and exposure suffered while on an exploring expedition in the mountains of that Territory during the winter of 1869. Failing in these prospecting tours to find any mineral deposits of value, he never succeeded in restoring his wasted fortune, but died leaving neither money or possessions behind. For a number of years Comstock, as was the case also with many of his companions, made some money testifying in the courts of Nevada in regard to the early location of claims along the great lode that now bears his name, issues involving millions of dollars being sometimes dependent upon the testimony of these men.

Fennimore, "Finney," "Old Virginny,"

(for by all these names he was known,) the first mentioned being, no doubt, his true and proper cognomen, died in destitute circumstances near Virginia City, which was named after him, a couple of years after the outbreak of the Washoe excitement, a few of his old cronies having contributed to his support towards the last. His death was caused by advanced years and a rather free indulgence in alcoholic stimulants, a habit to which he appears to have been long addicted. As already stated, he received nothing for his interest in claims upon the great mother lode, nor did he, like many others, benefit by his knowledge of the locations first made along it, his demise having happened before any of the more important legal contests came on. Of all the original claim owners none fared so badly, in a pecuniary point of view, as "Old Virginny," a man who, in so far as there was any merit in being early on the ground, deserved to have profited from this circumstance above all others.

Peter O'Reilly,

who realized more from his Comstock claims, perhaps, than any other of the original locators along it, having in the fall of '59 received from John O.Earl and Judge Walsh $36,000 for his interest in the Ophir ground, had for several years before been a resident of the Washoe country. Besides mining, he also engaged in farming, having been the owner of a well cultivated piece of land, situated two miles below Dayton, on the Carson river. O'Reilly was a man of good appearance and possessed of more education and intelligence than most of his companions, though exceedingly visionary and at times supposed to be a little flighty on some subjects. He engaged in a number of unprofitable enterprises, among others the erection of a capacious and costly stone edifice, commenced in the fall of '59 at Virginia City, having been the first structure of large dimensions undertaken in that place. He did not live to see it finished, having died the next year in a lunatic asylum, very far from being the Croesus that, in his dreams of great wealth, he imagined himself destined to become.

McLaughlin, The Winters Boys and Hammack.

Patrick McLaughlin the same fall disposed of his Ophir ground to Morrison & Hearst for the trifling sum of $2,500, nor did he ever after succeed in raising any large stake out of Washoe. He left the country poor, and has of late been following the laudable but illy requited and uneventful calling of a sheep herder in California, a bonanza that yields him probably from ten to fifteen dollars per month of net profits. Of the Winters Brothers, John D., Joseph and Theodore, who at one time owned amongst them extensively in the best mines at Virginia City and Gold Hill, all are living on or near a large ranch owned by Theodore on Putah creek in this state. These boys removed with their parents from California to the "Eastern slope" some years before the discovery of the Comstock lode, having been residents of Washoe valley at the time of that event. They followed farming and freighting over the mountains, having belonged to what was in early times denominated the "bullwhackers' brigade." The mother of these boys was a woman of great energy and decision of character, and the sons took after her, exhibiting at times rather an excess of action and animal spirits. What with the sale and working of their mining properties, they made at first a good deal of money; but being no niggards, it went at the same time pretty freely, Theodore being now the only one of their number who has much property left.

A.G. Hammack, one of the primitive stock of miners on Gold canyon, managed to secure, partly by location and partly by purchase, considerable interest in the Central, Chollar and Yellow Jacket grounds, the 100 feet he held in the latter having been received from the owners for running a short open cut on the claim. He sold his interest in the Central for $20,000, got several thousand dollars besides for his other interests and left in the fall of '59 returning to his family in Alabama, who were said to have been in needy circumstances. Hammack enjoyed a good reputation among his companions for honesty and square dealing, and possessed many strong traits of character. He is reported to have been killed during the Rebellion, fighting on the Confederate side, though his advanced age, over sixty, renders this statement somewhat problematical.

VII

Brief Sketches of Washoe Pioneers, Continued.

John Osburn, who, as we have already stated, owned one-twelfth of the Ophir and one fourth of the Mexican ground, went to Western Utah at an early day, having been engaged in placer mining along Gold canyon for several years prior to the discovery of the Comstock lode. Being a native of Kentucky, he was known among his companions as "Kentuck," the claim at Gold Hill so named having been called after him. He was a large owner in this as well as in several other valuable locations besides those above mentioned, and was at one time worth a good deal of money. For his interest in Ophir, sold to Donald Davidson and General Allen, he received a handsome sum, though we do not recollect exactly how much.

Osburn, who was marked by that lack of thrift so characteristic of the first settlers on the "Eastern slope," parted with his money freely, and therefore, as may be well supposed, pretty fast, having been reduced at the time of his death to rather moderate circumstances. He died at Silver City, a small hamlet on Gold canyon, four miles below the town of Virginia, in 1864, his death having been caused by a fractured limb that failed to mend readily, hastened, it is said, by grief arising from an unreciprocated attachment unwisely cherished for a young woman with whom he met a short time before. It may seem improbable to some that one so long separated from refined society, and almost a stranger to female influences, should have been seriously troubled by a feeling of this kind. But it is notorious that this sort of partial exile is apt to render men all the more susceptible to the tender passion, many of these Washoe pioneers, after they had acquired some wealth, having given way to this weakness in a remarkable manner. Comstock, within a year after he received his money, was despoiled of the most of it through the machinations of an artful woman, several of his companions having in like manner been cajoled out of their money, and sometimes into hasty and ill-advised wedlock and that not always with women of the most exemplary of deserving kind.

Unhappy Effects of Suddenly Acquired Wealth on the Marital Relationship.

In some cases the staid and previously well behaved wives of these financially fortunate men took it into their heads, upon their husbands becoming rich, to play an imperious and overbearing part, persisting in which, they generally succeeded in securing the larger share of his effects, and in rupturing the marital bonds that had bound them together. It was so with poor Berry, whose spouse, (the supernumerary wife of a Washoe Mormon who had unsealed and set her adrift,) so soon as she had got fairly wedded, deftly relieved her loving and unsuspecting husband of all his spare cash, and then took her departure for the City of the Saints, leaving him to die poor and deserted. It was so with Wm. McNulty, once a well-to-do-merchant in Ohio, afterwards a prosperous business man in California, who went to Washoe in '60, put up a mill and made money, lost some of it, took to drinking, mistreated his wife, who left him, having first secured the fragments of this fortune, all of which drove the despondent and ruined man to commit suicide, which he did by shooting himself at the Eagle hotel, in Sacramento, in the year 1865. It was so with poor Joseph Hastings, whose wife left him, perhaps not without cause, and afterwards married J.R. Hardenberg, of San Francisco. Hastings sold out his interests in Washoe, which consisted of mining grounds, water franchises, arastras, etc., and realized from the same a handsome sum as

34

early as 1860. He died a few years after, old and quite poor, his wife, a nephew and some other parties having secured a portion of his wealth, and thus saved it from going as the most of it had already gone, without any resultant benefit to any one.

So also fared Hiram Bacon, once the owner of the famous Bacon Claim, now a portion of the Empire-Imperial ground, situated at what was long considered the very core of the Gold Hill bonanza. He owned also other valuable ground in the vicinity and became at an early day, through the sale of these properties, a man of large wealth, after which his evil star arose in the shape of a termagant and ungrateful wife, who having set herself systematically at work to plunder him, succeeded so well with the job that he was compelled at last to seek relief from his property and sufferings in the almshouse at Placerville, where he died a pauper only a few years after his unfortunate marriage. Other examples might be cited tending to illustrate the infelicitous effects of suddenly acquired riches upon that class of people to which these Washoe pioneers belonged.

In our next paper we will speak of a class of men the very opposite of those we have just been considering, for a few such were to be found in those Washoe silver regions almost from the start.

VIII

The Washoe Pioneers and Their Successors — Herman Camp and His Eccentric Fortunes.

Very unlike the men spoken of in the last number of these papers — the original locators of the Comstock lode — were their immediate successors, the parties who bought them out, paying what were at the time considered extravagant prices for their claims. Foremost among this more shrewd and better educated class of men was Herman Camp; not that he was the first to secure through purchase permanent ownership of a portion of the rich deposits on the great mother lode, this distinction being due to James Walsh and Joseph Woodworth, but Camp was the first to effect such a purchase, agreeing to pay for the interest secured a price denoting something like a proper appreciation of the worth of the new-found silver mines. Arriving in Washoe towards the latter part of July, 1859, Camp, who was a man of quick perception and possessed of a bold and speculative turn of mind, took in the situation at a glance and forecast the future of the county with wonderful correctness. He estimated the new ore find as being of the first importance, and rightly divined that an active mining industry would here grow up, requiring costly reduction works and a considerable town for its accommodation. Impressing these views upon other parties possessed of more money than their sanguine and eloquent adviser, he readily induced them to give him a contract for putting up a number of stone buildings in close proximity to the mines, no town site having as yet been laid out.

37

A Persuasive Talker.

Camp was not only an active, wide awake sort of person, but a most persuasive talker; the fact that he succeeded in causing Comstock, at their first interview, to deed over to him his entire interest in the Ophir ground for a moderate consideration, only one dollar of which was paid down, being sufficient evidence of his power in this respect. This transaction took place on the 6th of August, on which day the purchaser was duly installed into the premises and commenced taking out ore from the excavation already opened. That night Comstock, meeting with his companions, was so much badgered on the foolish bargain he had made, that he concluded, with their promised assistance, to go at once and take possession of the claim which he had, by a legally executed deed, transferred to another party, then in lawful and peaceable occupation thereof. This was accordingly done, and when Camp came in the morning to resume work he found the pit in the possession of an armed gang of ruffians, who threatened him with instant death should he attempt a forcible re-entry upon the ground.

A Fatal Mistake.

Being an eminently good natured and peace-loving man and feeling that he could by no possibility be in this manner ousted from his claim, Camp proposed that the matter be referred to a jury of miners, agreeing to abide by their decision in the premises, a proposition that his adversary readily acceded to, well knowing that he could give to this assemblage such a moral complexion as would insure a decision in his favor. The friends of Camp cautioned him against pursuing this course, pointing out the danger to which he would be exposed in doing so. Dr. Henry DeGroot, who had long been acquainted with, and knew him to be an energetic, honorable man, well able and likely to perform all he had undertaken in his contract with Comstock, advised him strongly against submitting the question of his right to retain the ground to any such sort of arbitration,

38

urging him to go at once to Genoa, the county seat, and put his deed on record, and then, if in fear of personal harm, to leave the country, trusting to the courts for the vindication of his rights, and the ultimate restoration of his property.

Not wishing just then to go away, and confident that but one result could be reached by the proposed tribunal, Camp preferred to submit to them the matter for settlement. As had been foreseen, this meeting, when it came to assemble, was made up mainly of Comstock's cronies, a whisky-sodden set, whose having already prejudiced the case, decided as a matter of course against Camp, who, in accordance with his pledged word, surrendered his deed and gave up the contest. In relinquishing the claim to this property the acquisition of a splendid fortune was defeated when already within his grasp. Camp afterwards acquired large interests in the Gould & Curry and other valuable ground on the Comstock lode, and but for attempting to carry too much and sometimes holding on too long, might have come out largely ahead; as it was his Washoe experiences benefited him but little in the end, his wealth when he came out having been reduced to the zero point, about where it stood when he started in.

James Walsh and Joseph Woodworth.

As already stated, these gentlemen bought no mining ground on their first visit to Washoe, which occurred in the latter part of June, 1859. At that time their attention was mainly occupied with the mines at Gold Hill, the rich and easy working ores of which induced them to put a series of arastras on Carson river for their reduction. Comstock had on various occasions importuned them to purchase his mining interests, but not until the 10th day of August did he succeed in making a sale to these parties, the conditions of which have in these papers heretofore been mentioned. They also soon after bought into several other claims, ranking before the end of 1860 among the largest mine owners along the Comstock. During that year Judge Walsh parted with the greater portion of his interests, realizing fair but not extravagant prices therefor. Woodworth, who held on to the most of his, became very wealthy, being able at one time to sell out for a million of dollars. Extending his operations at a period when labor and material were enormously high, and the methods of ore reduction were as yet both costly and imperfect, he met with heavy losses, and finally retired from Washoe with but a remnant left of his once large fortune. Judge Walsh, who undertook to treat the refractory ores of White Pine and other interior districts, erecting expensive smelting works for that purpose, also lost much money, coming out of the country where he had at first succeeded so well, with an exchequer even more seriously depleted than that of his enterprising confrere.

Among the Men Who Became Largely Interested in the Comstock Mines.

Almost at the start, visiting them in person or purchasing on the representation of others, the following embraces perhaps a tolerably full list: Donald Davidson, after whom, because of the active and intelligent interest he took in the development of the new silver bearing region, the most conspicuous peak in the Washoe range was named. General Allen, partner with Donald Davidson in the purchase of Ophir, the two being early and quite extensive buyers into that ground. George Hearst and William Morrison, the latter being for a time at first superintendent of the Ophir, William M. Lent and B.F. Sherwood, owning and afterwards operating jointly and pretty largely in Washoe properties. Richard Ogden and J. Downes Wilson, who bought freely at the opportune moment and, through judicious management, made a good deal of money, some of which was afterwards sunk in the erection and running of a mill, a perfectly legitimate but not at that day always profitable line of business. Erastus Sparrow and Joseph French, who bought the French & Sparrow ground at Gold Hill and soon after put up a large mill on the American ravine, which from the first proved and has for many years since been run as a successful concern. John O. Earl, Andrew B. McCreery, Alpheus Bull, all of whom got a good financial send-off through fortunate investments in Comstock ground. M.C. Hillyer, Henry G. Blasdell, afterwards Governor of Nevada, A.D. Perkins, Hiram Pierson, William F. Bryant, Louis Schloss, J. McKinry, E.S. Gross, William N. Thompson, H.H. Raymond, extensively engaged in ore reduction, with a disastrous ending; the man who long and worthily bore the most exalted of all titles, "Honest" John Atchison; J. Neely Johnson, Frank M. Pixley, who made the journey over the mountains on his famous mule in mid-winter, bought and, what was equally important, sold at the right time, adding materially to his already quite large and fairly earned wealth. There were, doubtless, others whose names should be included in this list, though we cannot just now recall them to mind.

Done With Earth.

Of the persons here enumerated the following are deceased, nearly all of them having died with fortunes considerably reduced and some of them quite poor: Herman Camp, Donald Davidson, B.F. Sherwood, E. Sparrow, E.S. Gross, William N. Thompson, H.H. Raymond, John Atchison and J. Neely Johnson, the two last mentioned having died at Salt Lake City, where they had gone, the first to look after mining, and the other to attend to some legal affairs.

IX

The Washoe Argonauts — How They Saved and How They Squandered.

Before proceeding to speak of the early developments made on the Comstock lode and of the first mills and reduction works put up for the treatment of its ores, some further, but brief, remarks may not be out of place concerning the fate and fortunes of the pioneer owners along that lode; a class of persons to whose histories the rare opportunities they enjoyed for acquiring large wealth have imparted an interest that neither their intrinsic merits nor any other incidents connected with their lives could ever have inspired. In other words, it is these fortuitous events rather than the men that awaken curiosity and prompt us to inquire what became of the individuals themselves. We naturally like to know what use men so situated made of their opportunities; suddenly and easily acquired riches producing often very unlike effects upon the human mind, as is exemplified in the story of these Washoe pioneers, some of whom made the most of their good luck, economizing and adding to their gains until they became millionaires, while others (and this was much the largest portion of them), recklessly spending their money as fast as they received it, remained as they had always been, impecunious, shiftless and generally indebted to all who would trust them. A few of them were men of education and refinement, reticent, cautious and thrifty; more, however, were garrulous, imprudent and spendthrift; almost the whole of them being men of generous impulses, free-hearted, and even liberal towards their friends or those whom they happened to like, to a fault.

The first parties who realized any money from the Comstock mines were

The Owners of the Small Rich Claims at Gold Hill,

where a number of arastras were being profitably run several months before the silver bearing deposit in the Ophir ground was opened or even discovered. These Gold Hill claims, beginning on the north, consisted of the following, applying to them the names by which they were latterly and more generally known: The Triglone, 31² feet; the Imperial-Empire, 123 feet; the Bacon, 45 feet; Empire North, 55 feet; Eclipse, 30 feet; Trench, 20 feet; Empire South, 20 feet; Plato, 10 feet; Bowers, 20 feet; Piute, 20 feet; Consolidated, 51 feet; Rice, 13 and one-third feet; Imperial South, 65 and two-thirds feet; Challenge, 50 feet; Confidence, 130 feet; the most of these claims being now covered by the ground of the Imperial-Empire Company. Small as they were, the majority of them were shared by two or more partners, their extreme richness justifying such sub-division of ownerships. With the transfer of these properties that frequently took place, they often changed names, being sometimes known by one name and sometimes by another.

Among the principal owners in the claims along at first was

Alexander Bowers,

generally known as Sandy Bowers, owner of the ground that bore his name. Though of Scotch descent he hailed from Missouri, whence he came overland and, tarrying on the Eastern slope, had been following the business of placer mining along Gold canyon for several years, when the notable silver find occurred. He was a rough, honest fellow and well liked by his companions, though not so canny and circumspect in his wordly affairs as his countrymen are commonly reputed to be. He owned originally but 10 feet on the main lode, the additional 10 having been the property of his wife, acquired by her before their marriage. Mrs. Bowers was also of Scotch origin, a hard working, industrious body, who, having repaired to the little hamlet of Gold Hill in the spring of 1859, was there living in a very rude and comfortless sort of abode as late as the month of August of that year. She did the washing for the miners, a business that paid well at that day, there being, as yet, no Chinamen in the country, and had gathered not a little gear prior to her marriage with Sandy.

Bowers' claim proved very rich and he made a great deal of money along at first. Afterwards he built a large mill near his mine, and still later a splendid mansion over in Washoe valley. The mill was not a success, which, with some pecuniary reverses afterwards sustained, reduced his accumulations materially prior to his death, which occurred some 10 or 12 years ago at his residence in Washoe. His widow still lives and is reputed to be endowed with something of that occult power that enables the possessor to foresee future events. In the exercise of this faculty she has frequently prognosticated ore developments on the Comstock, some of which are said to have been verified by subsequent events.

Joseph Plato

was the owner of the once well known Plato claim, which, although it contained but 10 feet, turned out for some time a large amount of extremely high grade ore, having been even richer than the Bowers ground, which it adjoined on the north. Plato was a man of extraordinary physical powers, and although not a professional athlete, was much addicted to feats of skill and strength, having, as is apt to be the case with men so constituted, injured himself by over-indulgence in exercises of this kind. He was an early resident of Washoe, and obtained his ground at Gold Hill for a trifling consideration. He was one of the few of those pioneers who not only made money, but possessed the faculty of keeping and employing it to advantage. He died in San Francisco about 10 years ago from general debility, his death having been hastened by a wound caused by the bursting of a gun, while on a visit to Carson valley. His widow, who was left in good circumstances, afterwards married Mr. Howard, now one of the rich men of the city.

John Newman,

who was part owner in several good claims, one of them situate at Gold Hill, put up the first permanent house erected on the site of Virginia City. This was a stone building and was completed in the month of August, 1859. It afterwards enjoyed the infamous distinction of being the house on which the first and only secession flag ever hoisted in Nevada was run up. This event happened in the spring of 1861, and came well nigh costing the proprietor his life. In this house Newman shoftly after killed a man, and, as it was at the time alleged, without any sufficient cause or provocation. As the country was then without courts or law, no notice was taken of the crime. This man was a tailor by trade, but honored the calling by leaving it and betaking himself to less reputable pursuits. He came to San Francisco a few years after the discovery of the Washoe mines, and there married a woman greatly his superior, being a person of some education and pretentions to literary taste. He died soon after, leaving some real estate but not much money behind. Of

James Rodgers

very little is known. He was quite a young man, was in the country when the silver mines were discovered, and obtained interests in many valuable claims at both Virginia City and Gold Hill. He was also largely interested in the Flowery district, then considered a promising mining locality. Rodgers was noticeable for his quiet and retiring habits, and without being intimate with any, stood well in the estimation of all who knew him. One morning in the summer of 1860, he was found dead in his room in Virginia City, shot through the head by a pistol ball. Whether it was a case of suicide or assassination never was ascertained. The fact that he had no enemies seemed to favor the theory of self destruction, while the still stronger fact that no trace could be found of his money or other effects argued that he had been murdered by parties who had already taken measures for securing his property, knowing that in the loose state of society that prevailed no very searching inquiries would be instituted as to the manner or causes of his untimely taking off. If Rodgers had any friends living the fact never came to light, nor did they probably ever receive any portion of his really valuable estate, this having in some mysterious way been absorbed by strangers.

X

Coppers and Mills.

Among other original or very early owners in the various small but rich claims at Gold Hill were Paul Coppers and John H. Mills, proprietors of what was for a time known as the Coppers & Mills ground, which for several years made a large and profitable production. Joseph Webb, an assayer by profession, owned one half of Coppers' interest, the two being joint proprietors of and running a saloon at Gold Hill meantime. Webb passed from the earth plane a good while ago, and if he has since been keeping company with Dives, it will not be because he died possessed of the riches imputed to that unhappy personage. Webb's estate was by no means hurtfully large, having barely sufficed to defray his funeral expenses and make his accounts square with the world. Coppers also suffered a financial collapse, after which he emigrated to Idaho, where he is said to have again made some money. John H. Mills still lives at Gold Hill, where he continues to be interested in mines and mining affairs, his fortunes since the period we are speaking of having fluctuated widely. At times he has been accounted rich, and is now said to be at least tolerably well off. He enjoys the reputation in the community where he lives of being a man of integrity, energy and first-rate business capacity. He is one of the most popular men in Nevada, having held a number of high official positions, among others that of Speaker in the lower branch of the State Legislature.

The Eclipse Ground,

covering 30 feet on the richest part of the Gold Hill bonanza, was purchased from Comstock in 1859, by Wm. and Alexander Henderson, brothers, who that summer arrived in Washoe overland from Missouri, two of their companions, named Allen and Hudson, having afterwards become equal partners with them in the ownership of this property. The consideration paid Comstock for this piece of ground, consisted of an old horse and $40 in money. Being unacquainted with the business of mining, these men, notwithstanding the low price at which they had bought their claim, ran themselves in debt in their attempts at working it. The following year DeLand, who had advanced them considerable money to enable them to keep operations in progress, took the management of the mine, seeing no other way to save himself from loss. At first the ore which paid well was reduced at custom mills; when funds enough had in this manner been accumulated a mill of their own was put up, the net earnings of which sufficed for a long time to pay a monthly dividend of $25,000, being $5,000 to each proprietor, DeLand having by this time become a one-fifth owner. In 1861 Allen was killed, having been shot through the head while prospecting near the town of Aurora in the State of Nevada. Alexander Henderson returned to Missouri. William, his brother, married in Washoe and afterward settled in San Jose, California, where he has a fine residence and is now living, being in good circumstance; Hudson we have lost sight of and DeLand is a denizen of San Francisco, still actively engaged in mining, milling and kindred pursuits.

Logan and Holmes

bought, in the summer of 1859, a section of the rich ground at Gold Hill, which so long as they continued to own it, went by the name of the Logan & Holmes claim. In the fall of that year they put up several water-driven arastras on Carson river, near the site of the present town of Dayton then called Chinatown. The next year they erected on this spot extensive reduction works, and for awhile prospered and made money. The cost of these works, coupled with an unfavorable turn in their mine and some other untoward events led to a turn of luck, and finally to such embarrassments that the most of their property passed from their hands, leaving them comparatively poor. Holmes, during his prosperous days, married a young wife, but survived this event only a short time, having died in 1865, leaving little money or property behind. Logan still lives and has, in the role of prospector and miner, been for many years past pursuing the fickle and fugacious Goddess of Fortune in the mountains of central and eastern Nevada without being able to quite overtake her. At White Pine he caught a glimpse of her vanishing form, and afterwards at Pioche actually laid his hand upon her, but somehow she managed to elude his grasp. The active and persevering Logan is not, however, the man to give up, and will yet possess himself of a fair share of this world's lucre if only his lease to earth life shall be renewed for a year or two longer, as he is said to own some very promising locations which only require a little capital to make their wealth practically available.

Of all these early-day Gold Hill nabobs, none were more heard of at the time, nor did any scatter their money with a freer hand, than

John Harrold,

who, with his partner, John Drynan, owned one of the best claims at this famous locality. Born at the South, and bred to the business of overseer on a large slave plantation, his naturally frank and generous disposition was apt to manifest itself in such an imperious way as often involved him in trouble with others. It was this sort of schooling that led him, on the outbreak of the late civil war, to take such a pronounced stand on the side of the South, that the United States authorities felt compelled to arrest and imprison him; a proceeding that greatly exasperated him and his friends at the time, but which Harrold himself did not afterwards very strongly condemn. For two or three years he realized from his claim a great deal of money, but, having one or two actual and perhaps many more "quasi" partners, with hosts of boon companions, political confreres and

51

hangers-on, amongst whom he shared his income freely, he failed to get much ahead, even while his mine was yielding princely revenues. With deeper working the ores depreciated in value, while the cost of extracting them rapidly increased, and but few years elapsed before Harrold, with his lavish expenditures, was forced to part with his ground; and, although he still retained an interest in several other claims about Gold Hill, they failed to replenish his coffers; and his old friends falling away or being unable to assist him, he was finally borne on one of those tidal waves of excitement that occasionally swept over Nevada across the deserts towards the east, fetching up at last with the great army of the dead broke upon the Pogonip-enveloped hills of White Pine, where he became enfeebled in health and utterly cleaned out in purse. After drifting about for a while in that desolate region, aided by some friends, he joined a party that had been formed for working the gold mines of Honduras. This company are said to be meeting with fair success, and expect in the course of a year or two to take out a good deal of money. Harrold, being in feeble health, does the cooking for his companions and thus manages to maintain his interest in the concern, and, should his life be spared, it is not improbable that he will once more partially recuperate his fortunes and return to the scenes of his former successes and failures. Drynan, his partner, who was a different style of man, saved some money and returning afterwards to California, bought a homestead and settled in Oakland, where he is now living, having for some time past held the position of usher in the mint.

XI

The White & Murphy Ground

was located by Alexander White and John Murphy, Washoe miners of the ante-Comstock era. Their claim, which covered but 210 feet, now forms a part of the Consolidated Virginia mine. They sold out early, realizing but a few thousand dollars for ground that has since been sold many times over at the rate of more than fifty thousand dollars per foot, or ten million dollars for the whole. Both of these men are now dead, White having died many years ago, and Murphy more recently, both being poor at the time of their decease. Murphy, besides his interest in the above ground, owned at one time 200 feet in the Crown Point and some other locations at and below Gold Hill. But from none of these did he ever receive much money, having disposed of his interests therein before any important developments were made upon them. During the Reese river excitement he migrated to that country, and was there again fortunate in getting into a good claim, having been one of the locators and a fifth owner of the Murphy mine, situated in the Twin River district, 50 miles south of Austin. In 1864 he disposed of his interest in this property for $10,000 cash, after which he made a journey East, but does not appear to have remained there long, as he subsequently turned up among the advance prospectors at White Pine. But here his usual good luck failed him, and he, like thousands of others, was forced to leave the district with a depleted exchequer; nor, speaking in miner's parlance, did he ever again suceed in making a *raise*. Murphy, who was an Irishman by birth, was a man of considerable shrewdness and natural ability, and with better early opportunities and more favorable surroundings would

53

likely have achieved a larger and more permanent success. Being big-hearted and sociably inclined, his character was marked by some of the infirmities common to generous natures, such as a disposition to trust to luck and to spend his money freely among his companions and friends.

The Hale & Norcross Claim,

containing 400 feet on the main lode, was originally taken up by the men whose names it bears; both of whom were living in the country at the time of the Comstock discovery. Hale was an old man and a Mormon, having come from Salt Lake and settled in Washoe valley some eight or nine years before that event. He was about the only one of that sect, many of whom were then living in the valleys of western Utah, lucky enough to secure an interest on the great mother lode by location, though quite a number of "Jack Mormons," a class of Gentiles so called because of the special regard they manifested towards that people, had the good fortune to obtain claims or parts of claims in that manner. After selling out his ground in 1860 the old man returned to the Land of the Saints, where the $2,000 or $3,000 he had brought with him soon found its way into the plethoric purse of the church.

Norcross, who had spent most of his life on the ocean, acting in the capacity of a common seaman, had by some chance current of fortune been carried over the Sierra Nevada, and was, during the summer of 1859, at work in a sawmill standing at the head of Eagle valley. Excepting one idiosyncrasy he was not a man to be specially noticed or remembered — Norcross was one of the most profane persons we ever met with; and we say this not wishing to disparage the well-founded claims of other nautical men to great accomplishments in this direction. We don't say, as is so apt to be said in cases of this kind, that every other word this fellow uttered was an oath, because, in fact, it was not; yet we do affirm that he was noted for his impious and irreverent utterances, even among the primitive crop of

Washoe miners; and that these latter were by no means a God-fearing or, for that matter, a devil-fearing people, it is needless to allege. He joined Hale in disposing of his claim and soon after left Washoe and came to San Francisco. What became of this son of Neptune, if still alive, we know not; what has become of him, if dead, we know well enough. It is said that after having, sailor-like, spent all his money in fast living, he again betook himself to a seafaring life — a course he would be very apt to pursue on finding his coffers empty and his craft fast drifting on a lee shore.

The ground disposed of by these two men in the summer of '60 for some five or six thousand dollars, is now selling at a valuation of about three million dollars, and has in times past sold at much higher rates, if we deduct the cost of development and permanent improvements since made upon it.

John Bishop,

who was a Canadian by birth, went to Washoe in '58, mined along Gold canyon and ran much with Sandy Bowers. He owned at one time in Yellow Jacket, Crown Point, and other claims about Gold Hill. He also owned 50 feet, being one-sixth of the California ground now included in the great bonanza mine of that name. He procured all these interests by original location, his name appearing often on the old records of the Gold Hill district. Although he sold out early and at low figures, the amounts received from his various claims aggregated at a handsome sum. Being a man of many acquaintances and of social habits, his money went freely; and although an active prospector and good worker, we believe he has met with no special success since he left Washoe; his time of late years having been spent mining in California, or in tours of exploration into more distant parts of the country.

Bishop's name has recently been brought into prominence through its connection with a lawsuit instituted by certain Washoe parties against the present California company for the purpose, as set forth in their complaint, of recovering the 50 feet of ground formerly owned by him, and to which they allege the company have no legal title, the deed purporting to convey it to them, and through which they claim to derive title, being a forgery. As to the merits of the controversy we have, in its present stage, no means of judging, though the plaintiffs stoutly affirm that they can maintain their allegations by ample and incontestable proofs. If this is the case, it is a little singular, to say the least, that a suit for the recovery of this valuable estate should have been post-poned to so late a day.

XII

Emanuel Penrod,

who owned, at one time, a sixth of the Ophir ground, besides valuable claims at Gold Hill, came overland from Illinois and settled in Washoe early, having prior to the Comstock discovery never been in California. He took up a ranch on Clear creek, a few miles south of the present site of Carson City, where he spent his time between cultivating a small tract of land and placer mining, which latter calling he followed on the bar at Chinatown, and along Gold canyon. He was among the first to obtain a foothold in the new silver mines, the value of which he seems to have appreciated from the first. Being, however, a cautious and prudent man, he disposed of nearly all his interests early, realizing only moderate figures for the same. For his one-sixth share in the Ophir, sold to Judge Walsh, he received $6,200. He remained on his ranch for some time and until it became quite valuable, when he disposed of it and removed to Elko county, Nevada, where for several years past he has been engaged in hydraulic mining, and, according to report, doing remarkably well. Penrod always enjoyed among his neighbors and those who had dealings with him, an excellent reputation for honesty and good sense. He was also a person of fine courage and superior business qualifications, being, in fact, a good type of the straight-forward, enterprising Western man.

V.A. Houseworth.

Like Penrod and other settlers in western Utah, this man, tempted, while on his way overland to California, to tarry and try his luck in the placer diggings along Gold canyon, or to turn aside and seek refreshment for his famished stock and jaded teams in the grassy valleys

57

that lie along the foot of the Sierra, remained through the approaching winter and finally made up his mind to stop altogether, converting what was at first intended as a mere sojourn into a permanent settlement in the country. Houseworth came from western Pennsylvania, and being a blacksmith by trade, settled soon after he arrived in the country at Gold Hill, where he found profitable employment shoeing the horses and sharpening the picks of the miners. Being a man of intelligence, steady habits and good character, he was elected first recorder of the district. He owned in the Yellow Jacket and other claims about Gold Hill, and also one twenty-fourth of the Ophir, which last he disposed of for the sum of $2,000, Judge Walsh and Dr. Ober, an old and well-known resident of San Francisco, being the purchasers. The various mining interests which he parted with in 1859-60 for $3,000 or $4,000, would have brought him $500,000 or more had he held on to them a year or two longer. Having made a little "stake," which no doubt seemed to him a great deal of money, Houseworth returned to his old home soon after; and, although he came back to Washoe a few years later, he does not seem to have remained long. The probabilities are that he saw little opportunity, under the changed condition of things, for a man like him to further increase his "pile" or make another raise, and so betook himself again to a country where the chances for realizing a fair return for his labor were more certain, if not quite so tempting.

Naming the Mines — History of their Etymology.

In a majority of cases the names applied to the original locations on the Comstock lode require no explanation, the terms themselves, though in many instances wholly fanciful, sufficiently indicating their derivation and meaning. Of the 43 claims that may properly be referred to his class, 26 have been named in accordance with the rule here mentioned, 17 bearing the names of the parties who took them up or bought them from first hands soon after they were first located. Those at all conversant with this branch of etymological history need now be told how whimsical and even absurd are sometimes the primary reasons that operate upon the mind of the prospector when selecting names for his mining locations; hence the far-fetched and fantastical appellations so frequently given them. In the Comstock vocabulary this absurd style of nomenclature is not conspicuously apparent, the terms Ophir, Bullion, Exchequer, Challenge, Confidence, Empire and Imperial, as suggestive of certain ideas and properties, being appropriate enough; nor can any exception be taken to the remainder of this class, though not so happily chosen as the above.

The Allen and the Mexican Grounds.

We have already spoken of the fate of Allen, locator of the ground lying between the Utah and the Sierra Nevada, in which he was at one time largely interested and which still bears his name. The Mexican mine was so called after the Maldonado Brothers, two Mexicans who bought it in 1860 and afterwards worked the ores by the patio method, preparing at Virginia City and extensive yard with many arastras for the purpose. These were the only works ever erected in Washoe whereat this plan of ore reduction was practiced on a large scale. The Maldonado's were skillful miners in their way, working their ore more closely than was generally done by others at the time. They made money, and finally sold their mine to Alsop & Co. for a good price, after which they returned to their native country. This piece of ground went for a long time by the name of the Spanish claim, and is so designated on the earlier maps, the Mexicans being indifferently called Spanish, referring to the nationality of their ancestors and the language they speak, as the Americans are for the same reasons called English.

XIII

The Central, Kinney and Sides.

The Central ground was so denominated from its position between the Ophir and the California mines, then considered the most important, and in fact, about the only two claims, except the Mexican, worth much on the great lode. The Kinney ground, though not located by, was purchased at an early day by the man whose name it bears. After holding it for a long time, during which very little work was done upon it, he finally disposed of it to James C. Flood, for the sum of $1,200. Recently, Kinney has brought suit to recover a portion of this ground, which he alleges was deeded away by him under a misapprehension as to the number of feet he was actually conveying to the purchaser. This fraction of his claim now incorporated in the Consolidated Virginia mine, is worth in the stock market nearly a million dollars. Richard Sides, his brother William and some of their neighbors, managed, like many of the primitive settlers in Washoe, to possess himself of a section of the great mother lode on terms that involved the payment of very little money. This section, formerly known as the Dick Sides claim, covers five hundred linear feet, lying between the White & Murphy on the north, and the Best & Belcher on the south. It had not been much developed up to the time of its purchase by the owners of the Consolidated Virginia mine, of which it at present forms a part. Sides and his partners disposed of their interests in it many years ago, receiving what was then deemed a fair equivalent of the property. This man, who was living on Clear creek, Carson valley, before the discovery of the silver mines, still continues to be a resident of Washoe. In 1859, his brother William killed a man named Jessup, at the town

61

of Gold Hill, for which offense he was obliged to flee the country, the circumstances under which the act was committed being too atrocious for even a Washoe community to overlook. Jessup was buried close beside the wagon road at the lower end of the town, his being the first grave in the place. After a year or two his remains had to be taken up, the wagon road having been so changed that it ran directly over the little mound under which they rested. Jessup was held in good repute, and his death was much deplored by those who know him. He owned fifty feet in the Ophir at the time he was killed, from the sale of which his mother, who came out from Missouri soon after, realized a handsome sum.

Abernathie and Baldwin, who also lived on Clear creek, where they carried on ranching and lumbering, owned between them 150 feet in the Sides ground. Taking the money received from the sale of this property, and some feet they owned in the Belcher, they came over to California and bought land in Suisun valley, where they have since lived in independent circumstances.

Concerning the Locators of the Best & Belcher

we have not much knowledge. Best seems to have retired from the active scenes of Washoe life at an early period. Belcher, who had been a ranchman in California and went to Washoe in 1859, also disposed of his interest betimes, both in this claim and in some others at Gold Hill, which he had obtained from Comstock. Soon after he returned to this State and betook himself to his former occupation, which he has since successfully pursued. He was a quiet, gentlemanly sort of man, of more than ordinary intelligence and good business habits.

The Gould & Curry Claim

passed into the hands of these two men and their

associates early in the summer of 1859, having been sold to them by the original locators. The purchasers themselves sold out the same fall to other parties, and at low figures, Curry having received not over six or seven thousand dollars, and Gould still less for his interest. They were both men of superior character and first rate business capacities. Abram Curry, or as he was more commonly called, Colonel Curry, had been in early life a steamboat man on the Western lakes and rivers, and was marked by something of that off-hand, rough energy and frankness characteristic of men trained in that school. He was, nevertheless, a kind-hearted, honest man, and distinguished for his public spirit and enterprise. He was among the first settlers at Carson City, and did more than any other man to build up and improve that place. As early as 1860, he took up the Hot Springs, two miles east of the town and put them in fit condition for public use. At this point he also opened extensive stone quarries, from which he afterwards took out material for the construction of a court house and other public buildings, at Carson, and still later for the Capitol of the State, and the United States mint, all of which were put up under his supervision. He also held the position of Superintendent of the Mint at that place, the duties of which he discharged in a manner to secure the approval of both the Government and the people. He died at Carson City some four or five years since, leaving his family not exactly poor, yet far from being rich. His partner Gould went to Reese river in 1862, and there engaged in the lumber manufacture and trade, which he carried on successfully for a number of years. Later, he was at several of the other pioneer mining camps in central and eastern Nevada, engaged in the same line of business. He is now a resident of California, and it is not too much to say of him that he has always enjoyed the confidence and respect of the several communities in which he has lived and transacted business.

XIV

Savage,

who has been a miner at Downieville, went over the mountains in the summer of 1859. Soon after his arrival at Virginia City, he, in conjunction with two or three others, bought the ground that now carries his name from a party of "jumpers," satisfying at the same time the demands of the contestant claimants. In 1860 he was engaged in packing goods over the Sierra, but soon after disposed of his mines and having some money, came to California, where he purchased land, upon which he has for many years resided, a staid and prosperous farmer.

William Chollar,

whose name is connected with the Chollar Potosi, was also a California miner. He went to Washoe in the fall of 1859, located the Chollar ground, in which he held the usual two-hundred-foot claim, and undertook to explore it by means of a tunnel. This, though a costly work, availed nothing, therefore he sold out and taking the proceeds of the sale returned to his home at Grass Valley, and there again engaged in mining. He was a clear-headed business man, active and industrious, but being of a convivial disposition, at times spent his money lavishly. Some seven of eight years ago, at the earnest solicitation of his brothers living in Connecticut, he went home to that State, where he is reported to have since died.

Triglone, Trench and Overman.

John Triglone, once owner of the Triglone claim at Gold Hill, is now and for some ten or twelve years

65

agone has been a well-to-do quartz miner in Amador county, California. He did tolerably well over in the land of salt, sage-brush and silver, having, besides his mining ground, been a large owner in the Swansea mill, which for some time made handsome net earnings. The Trench claims, covering twenty linear feet in the heart of the rich shute at Gold Hill, was bought by Joseph Trench and Erastus Sparrow in the fall of 1859, these parties having the next year put up a large and well appointed mill at the mouth of American ravine, which was run for several years with large profits upon the ore taken from their mine. Sparrow, who was already an old man at the period we are speaking of, died several years ago. His partner in this enterprise still lives, an energetic, stirring man, as noticeable for his sturdy physique as for his kindly disposition and good natured bonhomie. He is supposed to be financially well off. Overman, the last in this category of names, (as this claim is also the last on the universally recognized line of the Comstock lode), belonged to the Washoe mining pioneers. This circumstance did not, however, profit him greatly, as he parted with his interest in the ground that bears his name for a trifling consideration. In the summer of 1859, he was living in a log cabin near this spot, a quiet, elderly man, still earning small wages in the nearly exhausted diggings along Gold canyon. He died in Washoe several years ago, and was buried near the scenes where he had so long lived and labored.

The Name and but Little Besides.

As we have seen, the various mines situated on the Comstock lode were named, for the most part, after the men who first took up claims thereon, or those who purchased from these original locators. Both of these parties, with a few exceptions, disposed of their interests at an early day, not a single one of the men whose names are attached to these mines having long remained a large owner in any of them. It is probably enough that these pioneers do not today own so much as a share in a Comstock mine, unless it be some of the very low priced ones. More than one-half of these men are, in fact, now dead, few of them while living having been distinguished for that foresight and thrift, without which scarcely any secure wealth.

The Men of Nerve and Courage Come in for a Share.

Before dismissing this branch of our subject it may, perhaps, be proper to mention still another class of adventurers, who, repairing early to these new-found silver mines, managed, without money or hard labor, to secure small and sometimes very considerable interest in some of the most valuable and actively productive claims on the great mother lode. These men belonged to that class, numerous in frontier countries and rough communities, who, preferring excitement and danger to the drudgery of hard work, are apt to be chosen to fill the offices of marshals, sheriffs, constables, etc., positions which more quiet and peace-loving citizens do not often covet, and for discharging the duties of which they are not always well fitted.

Now, for so it was, many of these pioneer claim-holders were a good deal this stripe of persons themselves, or a kind whose experience led them to readily sympathize with the bold and adventurous. Some of them, too, were a little uneasy as to the tenure whereby they held their possessions, being nothing loth to strengthen the same by an alliance with these practitioners under the shotgun and revolver code. Hence the transfer to these latter of divers and sundry feet in the rich claims at Gold Hill was a thing of frequent occurrence. As a general thing, these were not men of a noisy and turbulent manner or quarrelsome disposition, given to bluster and exhibitions of brute violence. On the contrary, they were more often noted for their quiet and even gentlemanly deportment, but of firm nerve and cool and desperate courage. Many of them had been engaged in deadly affrays, but these had mostly occurred in the discharge of their official duties, or, if of a personal kind, had not often been provoked by themselves.

Tom Peasley, John Blackburn and Tom Andrews

might be cited as good examples of this school of men. Blackburn was killed at Carson City, December, 1861, by Bill Mayfield, a desperado and gambler. He was at the time marshal of the Territory, Mayfield having been led to commit the assassination through apprehension of being arrested by the officer. The killing was done in the early evening, in a well-lighted and crowded saloon, and was an act of wonderful daring on the part of the murderer, who approached his victim openly and while surrounded by his friends, and stabbed him to the heart, after which he marched out, flourishing his bloody knife in defiance and made good his escape through the aid of confederates outside. Blackburn, as he saw his adversary approach, drew his pistol, and would probably have killed him, had not his own friends, by injudiciously interfering, defeated his purpose. With his last gasp he leveled his weapon upon the retreating assassin, but fell dead before he could draw the trigger, his eyes burning with a fearful desire for vengeance. Blackburn, when entirely himself, was averse to acts of violence, though one of the bravest men that ever lived. When excited with liquor, however, as occasionally happened, he was a most dangerous man, attacking, without discrimination, his friends and his foes. Only a few days before his death, being slightly under the influence of liquor, he assailed and would have killed Wm. M. Stewart on the streets of Carson, but for the prompt interposition of Thomas Hannah, then with Stewart, a member of the Territorial legislature. The provocation given for this deadly assault was not only trivial, but almost wholly imaginary. Mayfield, after being for sometime concealed in Carson City, and nearly perishing with cold, his limbs having been badly frozen, was arrested, but afterwards succeeded in making good his escape and fled to Montana, where he was killed in some gambling or other brawl a year or two later.

Peasely, while being the peer of Blackburn in point of courage, was at the same time a most genial, kind-hearted and companionable sort of person. He was also noted for his splendid physical powers, being at the same time a young man of intelligence, and by no means deficient in fine moral qualities. The incidents connected with his death were not very unlike those that attended the killing of Blackburn, the moving cause consisting in part of a personal grudge and in part of political differences. He, too, was killed in a saloon in Carson City, his assailant coming upon him unawares and shooting him fatally. With a pistol ball through his most vital part, such was the strength and will-power of the wounded man that he seized his murderer and, crashing him through a closed door, drew his pistol and deliberately shot him dead, falling the same instant, himself a corpse, upon the floor. Both Peasely and Blackburn had been quite largely interested in different properties on the Comstock lode, and were at the time of their deaths owners in some of the more valuable mines along it. Andrews, of whose name we have made mention, was also at one period interested in some of the Gold Hill grounds. After many rough and varied experiences these interests have slipped away, but the owner still survives, with seemingly a good many years of active service still in store for him.

We might adduce many other examples of men belonging to this class, but need not multiply them here, the cases already cited sufficiently illustrating the anomalous condition of affairs that made it possible for such valuable interests to be secured by considerations and services of the kind alluded to.

XV

Pioneer Mills and Millmen.

Postponing, for the present, further reminiscences of the first claim locators on the Comstock lode, and their immediate successors, who together gave their names to most of the mines along it, we proceed to remark briefly upon the first efforts made in the way of developing these mines and providing reduction works for the proper treatment of their ores. As already stated, the earliest attempts at working the Comstock ores were made in the spring of '59 at Gold Hill, the means employed consisting of the common Mexican arastra, some half-dozen of which were in use there before the rich ore deposit at Virginia City was discovered. During the following summer and autumn the number of arastras here employed was largely increased, several having been started near the site of the new discovery, and also down on Carson river, these last being driven by water. In the spring of 1860 the Maldonado brothers, owners of the Mexican, or, as it was then called, the Spanish ground, erected extensive yards for working their ores by the patio process, there having, as yet, been no mills or other reduction works put up here for the treatment of the ores.

Almarin B. Paul and the Introduction of the Washoe Pans.

In the month of March, 1860, Almarin B. Paul, an experienced quartz miner, and skillful metallurgist, of Nevada county, California, made a visit to the newly found silver mines of Washoe, and after carefully examining the character of ores, became satisfied that amalgamation could be thoroughly and economically

71

effected through the use of the iron pans already employed in the gold mines of California. This idea was rejected as absurd by the old school of metallurgists, all of whom contended for the use of the German barrel or the Mexican patio process, some even insisting that the ores here could be satisfactorily treated only by smelting.

So thoroughly, however, was Paul impressed with the adaptability of the pan process for this purpose that he instituted a series of careful trials directed to test the matter, the results of which fully confirmed his previous opinion. Satisfied that he was right, he determined that the mill which he had already concluded to put up in Washoe should be furnished with this and no other amalgamating apparatus. Having completed and organization styled the Washoe gold and silver mining company, No. 1, of which he was himself the moving spirit and almost sole director, Paul commenced on the 24th day of May, 1860, work on his new mill, which was located at a rugged pass on Gold canyon, known as the Devil's Gate, this site having been chosen because of its convenience to water.

The First Two Mills and a Close Race for Precedence.

On the 7th day of June, Paul gave his order to Howland, Angell & King, of the Miners' Foundry, San Francisco, for the iron work of this mill, which was driven by steam and carried 24 stamps. This machinery, with all needed supplies, was shipped over the mountains during the summer at an average expense of about $400 per ton, this being before any wagon roads had yet been constructed over the Sierra. As there was but a single saw mill then running in the country, the lumber required for this mill cost at the rate of about $300 per M, labor and material of every kind being proportionately high. Notwithstanding these and other obstacles, the projector and manager of this new enterprise pushed it ahead with such activity and vigor that he had the pioneer mill of Utah Territory advanced

72

so near to completion that steam was let on and machinery started up on the 11th day of August, 1860.

It was by a single point, however, that Paul gained this distinction for his mill, that of Coover & Harris, situated at Gold Hill, two miles above, having gotten up steam and set its stamps in motion only an hour or two later on the same day, as appears by the certificate of W.H. Howland to that effect, he having acted as engineer for both of these establishments on that occasion. As this was only an eight-stamp mill, the labor and cost of its erection were proportionately less, though the iron work, turned out at the same foundry, was not ordered until two weeks later than in the case of Paul's mill, which latter cost about $50,000.

Their Successful Career.

The two mills, though rude and unpretentious structures, compared with some of those soon after put up, had, nevertheless, a long and successful career, having made large earnings for the owners, while they served the mining public acceptably and well. Paul's first run was on Gold Hill ores, Alpheus Staples having given him a contract to work 4,000 tons, at $30 per ton, an arrangement that resulted to the mutual satisfaction and advantage of both parties. He had at the first endeavored to get a contract from the Ophir and the Gould & Curry companies, but they declined to furnish him with ore, being timid about his proposed method of amalgamation. Before his mill had been running a week, however, he had engaged to work ore to the amount of nearly half a million dollars, and so numerous were the applications thereafter, that he commenced, within three months, building near the town of Gold Hill another mill, which was to carry 64 stamps and cost $150,000.

The First Clean-up

made by him, amounting to several thousand dollars, was carried in iron kettles to Rhuling's assay office in Virginia City, where its appearance after being retorted created quite a stir, this being the first bullion produced in the country. It had, moreover, been demonstrated that pan amalgamation, since known as the Washoe process, would answer in the treatment of these Comstock ores, a fact that gave a new impetus to mining and imparted additional value to "feet." It is worthy of note that the first attempt at working the ores of the first silver mine ever found and opened in the country should have been attended with the inauguration of a process so distinguished for its efficiency and so essentially its own.

A Retort of Preposterous Dimensions.

Paul, entertaining a pretty high notion as to the richness of these Washoe ores, had taken over for use in his mill a retort of about 300 pounds capacity. This implement having been thrown out and for some days exposed to the public gaze, excited the jeers of passers-by who tauntingly inquired of the over-sanguine mill builder if he expected to ever fill the thing with amalgam. The first clean-up having more than filled this retort, put an end to these jocular remarks upon its extravagant dimensions. The retorts now in use at the larger Washoe mills hold several tons each, and it takes a good many of them to serve the purpose at that.

The Coover Mill

also ran at first for the most part on Gold Hill ores, the proprietors, Charles S. Coover and Dr. E.B. Harris, having contracted with Plato and Bowers to work their ore at $25 per ton. The building occupied by this mill was a mere shed, composed of tough lumber, and no one in passing by would have supposed it of much account. But the machinery was good, and it was run by a man who thoroughly understood and carefully attended to his business. Pass it at what hour you might and this mill was in motion, and so it continued for several years, giving the best of satisfaction to all who patronized it, while it enriched the owners. It afterwards passed into the hands of C.C. Stephenson, who also made money with it, but standing close to the wagon track, and proving to be quite in the main street of Gold Hill when it came to be widened and straightened, this venerable and useful structure was torn down and the machinery removed to eastern Nevada, where it was again set up and has since been pounding away as industriously as ever on the silver bearing ores of that region.

XVI

Pan Amalgamation, and What It Led To.

The trial of pan amalgamation having proved a success, demonstrating the facility and cheapness with which the Comstock ores could be worked, confidence in the value of the mines was greatly increased, and many parties were cnouraged to put up reduction works who would not otherwise have gone into the business. The popular idea that a vast deal of science, or at least much practical skill, was indispensable in the treatment of argentiferous ores having been thus partially dissipated, the California millmen were quite certain that they could deal with them successfully when a method so similar to that employed in reducing the gold-bearing quartz of this State would answer the purpose. Accordingly a good many of this class repaired to Washoe during the summer and fall of 1860, with a view to putting up mills and running them on this new school of ores. The arastras that had been set up the year before were designed merely for working the quartz found at Gold Hill, in which the most of the gold was free and easily separated, no effort having been made to save the silver which it contained; the miners not then suspecting, in fact, that it carried any of this metal. When the sulphureted silver ores of the Comstock proper came to be handled, this style of apparatus was found to be wholly inadequate; hence early recourse to more effectual methods became necessary.

Era of Active Mill Construction.

The completion in August, 1860, and the successful operations of the Paul and the Coover mills, was immediately followed by the inauguration of numerous

77

other enterprises of this kind, several having, in reality, been planned prior to the above date and in anticipation of the success that it was expected would attend these pioneer establishments. So rapidly, indeed, did this business of mill construction thereafter proceed, that no less than 86 works of this description, carrying a total of 1,200 stamps, and costing an aggregate of over six million dollars, had been finished and started up by the end of 1861, some 40 or 50 arastras and several patio yards built and set at work meantime, not being included in this estimate. Work upon a good many other mills had also been commenced before the end of that year, the most of which were completed early in 1862, when the era of most active mill construction terminated in so far as the Comstock mines were concerned, this industry having, for the next three or four years, been transferred to Esmeralda, Reese river, Pine Grove, Humboldt, and other interior districts.

Location, Cost and Capacity.

Of the mills built for reducing the Comstock ores eight, carrying 114 stamps and costing $200,000, were located in Ormsby county; six, carrying 106 stamps, and costing $1,200,000, were located in Washoe county; forty, carrying 573 stamps, and costing in the aggregate $3,700,000, were located in Storey county; twenty-two, carrying 360 stamps, and costing $1,000,000, were located in Lyon county, and ten, carrying 84, and costing $300,000, were located in Esmeralda county, there having been erected, up to the end of 1861, not more than two or three small establishments of this kind in any other portion of Nevada Territory.

The First Parties to Put Up Water-Driven Machinery,

east of the Sierra, for the purpose of ore reduction, were Judge James Walsh and his partner, Joseph Woodworth, who, on their first visit to Washoe, in the latter part of June, 1850, threw a slight dam across the Carson river, at a point about one mile above the present town of Dayton, then Chinatown, and, diverting the water into a side race, employed it for propelling a couple of arastras, which they constructed and put up there for testing the Gold Hill ores, they having bought from Comstock a small claim at that point before purchasing the silver bearing deposit a mile further north, and which afterwards constituted the site of the great Washoe discovery. The water right so secured on the river was, the next year, further utilized by the construction there of additional arastras and, finally, by the erection of extensive reduction works, this now being the site of the present Ophir company's large and efficient mill.

Besides Paul, Coover and Harris, the following parties commenced the erection of mills, and, in some cases, completed and had them running before the end of 1860: Richard Ogden and J. Downes Wilson, who, in November, 1860, finished the Ogden & Wilson mill, the first one completed in the Virginia City district; Henry G. Blasdel, Alpheus Staples, Israil W. Knox, who built the Olive Branch mill, Flowery district; McNulty, who built what was afterwards known as the Bacon mill; Peter Frothingham, who put up a small establishment on Carson river, four miles below Dayton; John B. Winters, connected with Woodworth & Mosheimer in the building of the Carson River mill; John Atchison, Logan and Holmes, whose works were also on Carson river; Trench & Sparrow; De Land, Eclipse mill; and various other persons, whose names we cannot now recall to memory. Among the mills that were begun this year and completed near the end of it or early in 1861, was that of the Spanish company, at Virginia City; the Aurora, Keller, Dayton; the Sproul and several other mills on Carson river, besides a number of small establishments along Gold canyon, one or two about Virginia City and several along Six-Mile canyon, in the Flowery district. In the next number of these papers something will be said about the Ophir, Gould & Curry and other extensive works put up in 1861-2 at an enormous expenditure of money, but which, after a few years, ceased operations and were finally dismantled, with some remarks upon the causes that lead to these disastrous results.

XVII

The Big Mills of Washoe — They Adhere to the Old Methods.

Notwithstanding the success of amalgamation by the pan or Washoe process had been fully established by the experimental trials made in the summer of 1860, as already related, such was the distrust of the new plan entertained by the Ophir, Gould & Curry and other of the leading companies on the Comstock, that they, acting under the advice of the old school of metallurgists, declined to adopt it in the extensive reduction works commenced by them in the fall of 1860 and finished the following year. Another reason for these companies sticking to the old and more expensive methods was the belief entertained by them that the great body of their ores was much richer than they afterwards proved to be; it having been supposed that an expense of $40 or $50 per ton for their reduction could well be borne, provided the work were so effectually done as to secure a very high percentage of the gold and silver they contained. How much these companies overrated the value of their ores at the start may be inferred from the fact that they offered, in the spring of 1860, to contract with Judge Walsh for the reduction of large quantities thereof at an average rate of $75 per ton, it not being their intention then to work anything of less value than this. Acting under these misapprehensions these parties projected their reduction works on an extensive and costly scale, these establishments in the subdivision of their departments, the elaboration of the ores, and, in short, in both completeness and details, conforming largely to European models.

The Mill of the Ophir Company

was put up in Washoe valley at a point 12 miles westerly from their mine, this site having been selected because of its proximity to wood and water and in the expectation that a railroad would soon be built between these two points. The buildings erected here covered an area of fully an acre, everything having been constructed on a grand scale. Besides the main edifice, an immense building was put up for the use of the patio process, which was here employed for a time on the poorer class of ores. Shops, stables, carriage houses, quarters for workmen, superintendent's residence, offices, etc., were all well built and capacious. The machinery, material and workmanship were also first-class, the cost of the entire hacienda having amounted to over $1,000,000. Besides the crushing mill, carrying 36 stamps, several furnaces for roasting or chloridizing the ores were provided, the Freiberg in connection with the patio process having been here practiced. Rows of huge barrels, used for amalgamating purposes and extending the whole length of the mill, were kept in ceaseless revolution. The services of 100 men were constantly required in the several departments, besides nearly as many more in cutting and hauling wood, making lumber, burning charcoal and other outside employments apart from those connected with the mines. A hundred tons of ore were worked here daily, independent of that disposed of by the patio method. In addition to the ground about their works the company owned 700 acres of grazing and agricultural lands lying in the valley near by and 9,000 acres of woodland on the adjacent mountains, where a saw-mill had been put up for cutting their own lumber. Over this grand establishment Captain William L. Dall exercised a general supervision, with Captain Henry A. Cheever for his assistant, both of these men having had a long and honorable service as commanders in our merchant marine.

The Ores Grow Poorer and the Works Cease to Run.

Thus situated, the owners of the richest section of the Comstock lode, and having within themselves everything requisite to work their ores to the best advantage, it was expected by everybody that the Ophir company was on the highway to sure and early fortune, and for a time their affairs really seemed prosperous enough. But their ores, which at first averaged about $150 per ton, soon began to decline in value, leaving under their expensive modes of manipulation, such a narrow margin for profit that they were obliged to supplant the same by the more cheap and simple but much derided Washoe pans, through the use of which they would no doubt have reached satisfactory results had not their works been located at such a great distance from their mine and had not the latter within a short time after this substitution been pretty well exhausted of its paying ores. As it was, this company, with all their bright prospects at the start, their valuable mine, extensive works and great facilities for ore reduction, achieved but a brief and moderate success; their expenses after two or three years having outgrown their income to such an extent that they found it expedient to close up their works, which, after their own ore supplies had failed, could not, owing to their remoteness, compete for custom work successfully with mills located nearer the mines.

The Final Collapse.

Having ceased operations and stood idle for a time, the business of dismantling this vast establishment was at length commenced, some of the machinery and more valuable material being disposed of to one party and some to another until its entire demolition was finally accomplished, the company having meantime disposed of most of their other property in the neighborhood. With the stoppage of the reduction works the considerable town built up around them was depopulated and speedily went to decay, scarcely a house being now left in the once flourishing city of Ophir to mark where it stood. The extinction of the town and of everything pertaining to it has been as utter as of the once promising industry which built it up.

The Gould & Curry Mill,

which was commenced about the same time and finished a little later than the Ophir works, surpassed the latter not only in size and cost of construction but also in style and perfection of finish. Possessing a property of great supposed value, the owners of this mine, the most of whom were men of wealth and liberal notions, determined that they would put up an establishment commensurate with the magnitude and importance of their mine and which should outrival anything of the kind ever before constructed in this or any other country, a purpose in which they were heartily and ably seconded by their general Superintendent, Charles L. Strong, also a man of large ideas, and by no means deficient in enterprise, energy and practical ability. With such a management, well supplied with money, the grand undertaking after being entered upon was pushed ahead rapidly, the site fixed for their structure having been a small flat at the junction of Six and Seven Mile canyons, two miles northeasterly of Virginia City. The spot was a rugged one, rocky and uneven, the cost of clearing away the ground and preparing for the foundation of the main building having amounted to more than had yet been expended upon any mill in the Territory. The massive walls laid for the reception of the main edifice, which was 250 feet long with wings 75 feet in length, all built of timber, were constructed of hewn stone, taken from a quarry near by, and dressed at great expense. The engine, of 150-horse power, a splendid piece of machinery, was built at the Pacific works, in San Francisco. There were eight batteries of five stamps each, capable of crushing 40 tons of ore per day. For generating steam to propel this engine, six furnaces with three boilers, each 26 feet long and 4 inches in diameter, with 14-inch flutes, were provided. In the various departments of this establishment, notwithstanding every labor-saving device then known in the business had been introduced, the services of 75 men were required working in relays day and night, operations here never having been intermitted. With its terraced walls and numerous out-buildings, the place bore something of the appearance of a fortified city.

And The End.

This company, like the Ophir, entertaining at first a great distrust of the Paul or pan process, employed at the outset the Tyler or Veatch plan of amalgamation, which involved the use of numerous deep tubs, the system being a mixture of the German, the patio and the pan process, which latter was after a time wholly adopted. The total cost of the Gould & Curry mill, all accessories and surroundings included, amounted to over $1,250,000, a good deal of this expenditure having been of a kind that would, with our present experience in the business of ore reduction, be considered superfluous, and some of which was even at that time by many believed unnecessary. The history of this grand and costly establishment was so similar to that of the Ophir that we need not here rehearse it in detail. After a successful career extending through a few years, the current expenses began to drag heavily on the company and the mine itself giving out, brought operations at last to a stand-still, after which the work of disintegration began and proceeding at rapid pace, has left only the massive foundations of the great mill to attest where it stood.

XVIII

Overdoing Matters at the Start.

Not only in the matter of mill construction did the pioneer miners on the Comstock greatly overdo things at the start. Their extravagant ideas about the mineral wealth of the country betrayed them into a variety of other equally fatal mistakes, such as the laying out of extensive cities at all supposed eligible points, the building of costly wagon roads over the mountains, the projection of gigantic tunnel schemes and the like, to say nothing of innumerable mining enterprises, backed by any amount of nominal capital. Within 18 months from the time that the Washoe excitement broke out more than a score of town sites had been surveyed at localities that were believed to possess such natural advantages as would speedily attract to them a large population, and render the lots there laid out exceedingly valuable. All the mineral and thermal springs within a hundred miles around had been seized upon under the impression that they could easily be converted into great sanitariums, whose wide-spread fame would at once attract to them swarms of invalids from every quarter. Through every pass in the Sierra Nevada between Sonora and the Downieville buttes a toll road had been commenced and partially constructed, nearly enough money having been expended first and last on this class of improvements to have built a narrow-gauge railroad over the mountains. Before the end of the year 1861,

Eighty six Companies, with an Aggregate Capital Stock of $61,500,000,

had been organized, the most of them having their headquarters in San Francisco, to open up and work the mines of western Utah, the era of excessively large capital and purely speculative mining having not yet been inaugurated. Only in one case, that of the Ophir, did the stock of any of these companies amount to as much as $5,000,000. That of the Gould & Curry, next in magnitude, was fixed at $2,400,000 and that of the Mount Davidson at $2,000,000, none of the other companies on the list having reached the latter figure, the most of them having ranged from $250,000 to $500,000. Of all the companies incorporated during that period,

Only Nine Survive.

Viz.; Ophir, Gould & Curry, Sierra Nevada, Chollar, Lady Bryan, Hale & Norcross, Utah, Bullion and the Daney, the limits of some of these having since been so curtailed, extended or otherwise altered as to nearly destroy their identity. The claim of the present Ophir company, for example, covers but a fraction of what constituted the original Ophir ground, while the Sierra Nevada, the Chollar and the Daney embrace a good deal more ground than they did at first; the Chollar having absorbed what was formerly the Potosi and the possessions of the Daney having been extended for more than a mile north of their original location. On the other hand, a good many small claims have been aggregated, constituting one or more large ones, as in the case of the California, Consolidated Virginia, Empire-Imperial, etc. Some of these incorporations, for one reason or another,

Enjoyed Quite a Fame in their Day.

The Burning Moscow, for instance, was for a time

rendered conspicuous through the long and bitter contest which that company waged with the Ophir, the problem of the one ledge theory having for the first time come up for adjudication and forming the turning point in the fight. The Mount Davidson company, formed to drive a tunnel into the Comstock lode and open it up to the depth of 1,000 feet, was for several years a live and popular institution, the end proposed having been then considered a marvelous undertaking. The Latrobe was another incorporation gotten up for a similar purpose, both of these companies expecting also that they would intersect some valuable blind leads in the course of their excavations. In this, however, both were disappointed, though the Latrobe company did have the good luck to strike such an amount of water as afforded them for several years a considerable revenue, this being a very scarce commodity at that period about Virginia City. Before either of these tunnels had reached their objective point, the Comstock lode had been opened to such depths by other means that, their further prosecution being deemed unexpedient, both were abandoned, causing severe disappointment to multitudes who had bought the shares of these companies, believing them to be a safe and profitable investment.

"Vanished into Thin Air."

It was the case, indeed, that very few of the many companies organized at this early day ever accomplished anything beneficial to the shareholders, nor did any considerable number of the other grand schemes then set on foot realize the fond hopes of the projectors. Not more than two or three of the many gorgeous cities lithographed and laid out ever advanced beyond that embryotic state. The medicinal virtues of the mineralized springs failing to be appreciated by the invalid public, these remained as before solitary Bethesdas in the desert. The most of the roads constructed over the mountains, being but little used, heavily burdened the slender finances of the counties and towns that had helped to build them, while of the mining claims located all over the country, not one in a thousand was ever able to make even a tolerable showing of mineral wealth. Of the multitudinous companies associated and incorporated, not more than a score or two have left any enduring record, all the rest having perished from lack of merit or sheer inanimation during their earlier stages of development. The "Hope" gave up in despair; the "Excelsior" failed to get any higher; the "Sucker," having drawn scant sustenance from the pockets of the hapless shareholders for a while, succumbed to its fate; the "Scoria" turned out to be dross; the "Naescharama" perished from some unknown cause, probably lockjaw; the "Great Republic" collapsed, and "Congress" adjourned *sine die,* the doom of these companies having been seemingly foreshadowed by their names.

The Ups and Downs of the Past.

In January, 1862, a great flood occuring carried off many of the mills situated along Carson river, inflicting severe loss upon both the millmen and miners, the entire damage sustained by these two classes having been estimated at $2,000,000. This event, in connection with the ill success that had attended the most of the prospecting enterprises engaged in, had a tendency to greatly depress the spirits of the mining community about this time. This despondency was, however, gradually removed by the developments that continued to be made on the Comstock lode, the mining interests of the country having been maintained in a prosperous condition for several years thereafter, when another season of depression and gloom ensued, to be followed in turn by an era of greater prosperity than ever before. From these events of the past a lesson of fortitude and patience should be drawn by those unfavorably affected by the stagnation now prevailing in the Comstock stocks, this ebb and flow of fortune appearing to be incident to the great Washoe lode.

XIX

They go Actively Into the Business of Exploring The Country and Locating Claims.

In the last number of these *Papers,* we were led to remark upon the manner in which the Washoe miners, through an over-estimate of the mineral wealth of the country, were at the start betrayed into many wild schemes and much prodigal expenditure. In nothing did this excessive confidence display itself more signally than in the expedition with which the region for many miles around was explored, the numerous mining districts that were organized, and the multitude of claims that were taken up. Not until the month of September, 1859, did the new crop of adventurers begin to arrive in the Territory in considerable numbers, and yet within 16 months from that time as many as 25 or 30 different mining districts had been formed, the country from Esmeralda to Humboldt, and from the base of the Sierra Nevada east for a long distance having been run over and settled with scattering mining camps. The area thus partially explored and populated amounted to some 10,000 or 12,000 square miles, while the number of linear feet located might be literally counted by the million. That not much attention was paid to the

Mineralogical Character of the Ledges Located

it is needless to say, very little pains having been taken to determine whether they were ore-bearing or not. It was enough that there was a ledge or the semblance of one, the inexperienced and excited prospector concluding that any, even the smallest and most barren quartz croppings, were worth taking up, if indeed they did not present conclusive evidence of valuable mineral deposits below. The more claims of whatever kind a man was able to get hold of, the better were considered his chances for making a fortune, or rather the greater the fortune he might be supposed to have already secured. Unacquainted with the character of silver-bearing ores and lodes, without the skill or means for making assays, every reef of rocks met with and sometimes even the boulders found on top of the ground were located under some fitting name significant of their supposed great wealth, the sole ambition of these prospecting "tramps" being the securing of numerous "feet," as attested by the certificate of the accommodating recorder.

What Led to this Extreme Activity, and Tended to Foster These Illusory Notions

of the vast mineral resources of the country, was the fact that the Comstock lode, which was made the standard for measuring the probable value of all others, was in no wise remarkable either in its surface dimensions or other external features. Its outcrop was neither large nor continuous, while the rich ores had as yet shown themselves at only two points along it. In the vicinity were other ledges to all outward appearance equally valuable; the Virginia, lying only a few hundred feet further west, presenting even bolder croppings at many places along it. The prospector found, in fact, fully as good looking ledges as this at Gold Hill and Virginia City wherever he went, wherefore it was not at all strange that he should, in his ignorance and inexperience, have attached to them an equal prospective value, and eagerly sought to secure as many of them as possible, and end that could be attained without much trouble or cost; and so the whole country was rapidly run over and locations made everywhere. It was unfortunate for the future of this industry that the business of silver mining amongst our people should have been inaugurated by the discovery of such an exceptionally rich lode as the Comstock proved to be, inasmuch as it led to an undue excitement at first, whereby both the miner and the general public were betrayed into all kinds of follies and prevented afterwards from exercising that degree of patience, industry and economy that would otherwise have been observed, rendering the business, most likely, a success from the start. Had we commenced on a lode carrying a low grade ore, we should have escaped the unhealthy excitement that ensued, while we would have been more apt to apply our labor and means with diligence and care in opening up the mines, satisfied to work hard and reap a moderate return. As it was, with our ideas inflamed and our expectations exalted to the highest pitch, we commenced building at the top, converting the business, as it were, into a pyramid standing on its apex instead of its base, hence much of the disappointment and disaster that followed.

Developments Delayed, and Disappointment All Round.

The winter of 1859-60 set in early and proved to be a long and severe one, wherefore but little work was done on any of the numerous ledges taken up the fall before. The cold and stormy weather continued with snow and sleet quite into the summer, in the early part of which the Indian war broke out, still further delaying the work that would otherwise have been done and postponing it for another year. Not until the spring of 1861, therefore, did the business of active development begin, after which another year was required to prosecute this work to anything like determinate results, and when these were reached they generally turned out to be unsatisfactory. Then came a reaction and for a time "feet" were in disfavor, till the glowing accounts from Reese river again revived the furore, and the business of prospecting for and locating claims became as active as ever, to be followed in a year or two by another decadence, and this by the White Pine stampede, which without ending may justly be considered the culminating point in these vein mining excitements, Schell creek, Panamint and latest and least of all, Coso and Darwin, having all been movements of a milder type.

XX

Filling Up the Geographical Vocabulary of the Country.

How rapidly a mining excitement, through a hastened influx of population, tends to multiply the names of natural objects and localities in a country before almost without any geographical vocabulary, the movement caused by the discovery of the Comstock lode aptly illustrates. Take any map of the region now constituting the State of Nevada, published prior to 1860, and we find it well nigh a blank. Scarcely more than 50 names, all told, appear upon it. The few mountain ranges, scattered at random over it, leave us to infer that the country is an almost uninterrupted plain, a supposition strengthened by the fact that it really does form a part of the Utah basin or Great American desert. The only rivers laid down are the Humboldt, Truckee, Carson and the Walker with their several forks in the northwest and the Rio Virgin and the Muddy in the southeast, these being, in truth, all the streams that exist here of sufficient size to be styled rivers. We see thereon the names of some half dozen lakes and sinks and sloughs. Dotted lines, devious and far separated, straggle across the nameless waste, indicating the trails of Fremont, Beckwith, Steptoe and other early explorers, while a single wagon road, coming in from the northeast, and following down the Humboldt, marks the route pursued by the pioneer immigration. Here and there is put down on these early maps a saline or thermal spring, a mud lake or a soda lagoon, the only towns or settlements appearing thereon, being the old Mormon station, now Genoa, Franktown, in Washoe valley, Ragtown, standing near Carson river, on the southerly edge of the Forty-Mile

desert and Chinatown, situate at the junction of Gold
canyon and Carson river, near the point where the old
immigrant road crosses the latter. Upon these early and
almost vacant charts, are put down neither townships,
counties, nor other political divisions; all that is in-
dicated in this direction being that the country
belonged to Utah Territory, being generally
denominated Western Utah.

Progress of the Work.

If now we look upon the map of this region, 18
years ago so nearly a blank, we find it crowded with
names. First, we have the Territory as an entirety
organized into the State of Nevada with fourteen
counties, some of which have been in part subdivided
into townships. A multitude of mining districts appear,
covering a large portion of the State, being those that
still maintain their organization, such as were formed
and afterwards disbanded through diminished population, or, as sometimes happened, through entire
desertion, having been dropped from the more recent
maps. Scores of towns and mining camps present
themselves, some of the former being of very respectable dimensions, both as regards business and
population; Virginia City and Gold Hill, which are
really but one place, containing about 25,000
inhabitants, while Carson City has over 5,000. Such
additional lakes and streams as have since been
discovered, as well also as the principal mountain
ranges and passes, the more noteworthy springs, the
borax beds and other remarkable salines have all been
looked after and duly named.

Scanty Material.

In this christening process the Washoe argonauts
have had to rely mainly upon their own lingualistic
resources, there having been here no previously ex-
isting Spanish and but a scanty Indian nomenclature, as
in California, to help them out. There were, to be sure,
names of aboriginal origin attached to some of the

96

higher peaks and ranges, and also to a few other of the more remarkable natural objects, but the adoption of these, except in a few instances, was by the whites deemed inexpedient because of their great length, their harsh and gutteral sounds or their awkward pronunciation. The Rio Virgin (already half anglicised), a small stream in the southeastern part of the State, and Las Vegas, meaning the meadows, in the same vicinity, appear to have been the only terms derived from the Spanish to be found on the early maps of all this region, the christening of these having been due to their lying along the old Spanish trail leading from Santa Fe to Los Angeles, and not because there had ever been any settlements made here by that people.

Of the Indian Names that Have Been Retained,

we have, first, *Tahoe,* applied to the large lake in the Sierra Nevada mountains, about two-thirds of it being in the State of California. The term, in the native tongue, means big or beautiful water, and adhering to the Indian rule should be divided into three syllables and pronounced Tah-hoe-ee, with the accent on the last, and not in two syllables, with the accent of the first, as we absurdly practice. The observance of the method mentioned besides being more in consonance with the analogy of the aboriginal tongue, would impart to the word a much more poetic and euphoneous sound. The newspaper press should attend to the correction of this mistake. Washoe, the name of an Indian tribe who formerly inhabited a series of valleys lying along the eastern base of the Sierra, is still retained, having been given to the principal valley in this series and also to the county which covers it, and the country adjacent. This term should have been applied to the State itself in accordance with the desire of many of the inhabitants at the time of its creation, as it had already become identified with the famous silver mines all over the world, and its adoption, apart from its eminent fitness and agreeable sound, would have prevented the many

97

mistakes that constantly occur through the confounding of this name and that of the large and populous California county adjoining this State on the west. The Truckee river was so called after the Indian who was employed by the Donner party to guide them over the mountains into California. He appears to have been a faithful and intelligent old man, and there is little doubt but these unfortunate people would have escaped the terrible fate that overtook them, had they paid attention to his timely warnings. Shoshone, Toiyabe and Toquima, names of three high mountain ranges in Nye county, are all of Indian origin; so also is Sinkavata, a broad valley lying to the west of the Shoshone range; Winnemucca, name of a town on the Central Pacific railroad, also of a shallow lake lying to the east of Pyramid lake, and connected with it by a slough, was the name of the principal chief of the Piutes, who lived to a great age, dying only a few years since, leaving a son who, succeeding to his name and office and who has, like his father, always maintained friendly relations with the whites. Pahranagut is the name of a mining district situate in Lincoln county, in the extreme southeastern part of the State. It once contained quite a large population and enjoyed a good reputation for mineral wealth, but failing to sustain it by practical results the place has, for years past, been nearly abandoned.

Having but a meager vocabulary upon which to draw, the early dwellers on the "Eastern slope" being those of the pre-Comstock era, managed to make this slender stock go a good way. Thus, the name of Kit Carson, the famous Indian scout and guide, was by them applied to a river, the pass in which that stream originated, the valley through which it ran, as well as to the lake into which it disembogued and the sink where the surplus waters of the latter finally disappeared; the name having at a later date been given to a county organized in this part of Utah, and afterwards also to a city, the now flourishing capital of Nevada.

Among the county names of the new State only that of Washoe is of Indian origin. Esmeralda county was called after the principal mining district within its limits. The term, meaning in Spanish an emerald, was in its application here a purely fanciful and not altogether happy one. Douglas county as named after Stephen A. Douglas, then United States Senator from Illinois. Ormsby, after Major Ormsby, an early settler in Carson valley and an energetic business man, who was killed while leading the expedition against the Indians in June, 1860. Storey in like manner was named after Captain Storey, who lost his life in the same expedition. Lyon was named in honor of General Lyon, a brave officer in the Union army, who fell at the battle of Wilson's creek, Missouri, in 1861. Churchill county was also named after a distinguished army officer, his name having before this been given to the fort, erected on Carson river in 1860. Humboldt county bears the name of Baron Von Humboldt, the great German scientist, traveler and author. Eureka and Elko were named after the principal towns they contain. Nye county was named after James W. Nye, first Governor of the Territory and afterwards U.S. Senator from Nevada, an honor that he well deserved. Lander after General Lander, of the U.S. army, who for many years was engaged in exploring the country between the Missouri river and California, and laying out wagon roads through the same. Lincoln county was named after the "martyr" President, and White Pine after the chief mining district of that region, the name having been originally suggested by a species of pine found in the neighborhood.

The towns and stations along the Central Pacific railroad were mostly named by the company; some, as Reno, Halleck and Wadsworth, after military men; others, as White Plains, Rye Patch, Wells, Palisade and Promontory, etc., from certain natural features or peculiarities of the place; while the choice of others, like Verdi, Vista, Toano, etc., was mere matter of fancy or taste. Mill City was a name applied to that site, now a railroad station, long before the road itself was built, it having been selected under the impression that the canal projected for taking water from the Humboldt and

99

conducting it to this point, would lead to the erection here of many mills for the purposes of ore reduction. The ditch never having been completed the mills failed, and as a consequence, the town also failed to be built.

The Twin Rivers.

When Fremont crossed this country in his expedition of 1845, he was led to notice while passing through Big Smoky valley two large streams of the purest water, issuing each from a narrow gate-like gorge in the Toiyabe range. These gorges are but a few hundred yards apart and the two streams continuing to flow out into the valley in close proximity and parallel to each other for quite a distance, suggested the name of "Twin rivers," which was accordingly given to them by the great "Path-finder," and they were so laid down in the maps afterwards prepared by him. When the inevitable prospector arrived in that region, recognizing in these two creeks the Twin rivers of Fremont, he adopted the name for a mining district, whence it came to be applied to a considerable section of the mountains and valley adjacent; the singular form of the phrase, "Twin River," having meantime come into general use.

Reese River

was named after Captain Reese, a Mormon, who having a home establishment at both Carson valley and Salt Lake, necessitating frequent journeys between these two points, was led to seek a shorter path than the circuitous route via the valley of the Humboldt. In carrying out this purpose he left the old immigrant road near Carson lake, and pursuing an easterly course came upon the small stream that now bears his name. Walker river and lake bear the name of one of the employees of the Northwestern Fur Co., who trapped on these waters many years ago. Pyramid lake is so called because of a high, conical rock rising from the deep water near its eastern shore. In looking over the modern map of Nevada, many streams will be seen there laid down as rivers, but they are with the exceptions already noticed, nothing but creeks, and the most of these very small creeks at that. Reese, Twin, White and many other so-called rivers, including the Virgin and the Muddy, are everywhere easily fordable, nor would it greatly trouble an active man to jump across almost any of them, except during their highest stages.

APPENDIX

The following from a recent number of the Virginia *Enterprise* will serve as an addition to the "Comstock Papers" published in this journal:

Yesterday morning the reporter was awakened from his matitutinal repose by the sound of picks and shovels near, and within a few feet of where picks and shovels first sounded on the Comstock. A moment later he found himself at the old original Ophir dump, near the intersection of Carson and Howard streets, the wind flapping his shirt sleeves fitfully and mussing his unkempt hair as he stood watching some Mexicans undermining the dump. It may be said, by way of explanation, that nearly the whole of the old dump was removed to macadamize C street last fall. To reach the bottom, therefore, only requires now the sinking of a few feet, where previously it would have been necessary to have sunk from 12 to 20. The Mexicans, to the interrogations of the reporter as to their actions, gave the following explanation:

During the season of 1861, when the great freshet visited Sacramento, the Ophir was being worked for the rich ore of the croppings. This was not to be reduced by the rude appliances of the day, but was to be sacked and shipped on the hurricane decks of mules to California. Each mule load was worth from $1,000 to $1,200, so rich was the rock. At the time of that freshet, from 20 to 30 sacks of this ore had been taken out and was ready to ship. The flood came down through Ophir ravine like the waves of the sea, taking everything before it. Cabins and all sorts of mining works were swept away by its fury. It even took a brick building down on D street. The sacks of ore were never found afterwards. The leader of the gang, with hair and beard like the almond's snowy bloom, and who mined on the Comstock before it was ever seen by the original prospectors, said he was satisfied that the sacks were covered by dirt and debris near where they were digging, and where dumps had subsequently covered them still deeper. Now that the dumps had been so nearly removed, he expected to be able to find them readily.

The conversation having thus drifted into olden channels, and the company having been increased by the presence of John L. Moore, one of the veteran prospectors of the Comstock, the reporter drew his note-book and listened.

Mr. Moore (to the gray-haired Mexican) — Did you know Savariano?

Mexican — Yes. He mined up here (pointing toward the old Mexican works) 20 years ago.

Moore — He was a great prospector.

Mexican — Yes. He found this (meaning the Comstock); he and Maldonado. Then he found Cerro Gordo. He discovered ore out there at Austin, too.

Moore — Did you ever go with him on his prospecting trips?

Mexican — Yes. I was with him when he found the Cerro Gordo.

Moore — Oh, Ho! then you know something about the 40 loads of ore stolen from Maldonado?

The Mexican looked alarmed; glanced at the reporter, shook his hands, shook his head, and refused to talk any more. At a nod from Mr. Moore the reporter took the hint without waiting for a boot as a starting point, and left.

An hour later he made it very convenient to meet Mr. Moore and from him he got the balance of the story.

When the pioneers first came to this section they found Mexicans working the claim named after them, but which is now part of the ophir mine. The ledge from which this ore was taken has never yet been found by the Americans. In those days one-half of the claim was owned by Maldonado, and was worked by Savariano. The ore was very rich, a single mule load being worth from $1,000 to $1,200. This was taken by pack mules to California by the way of Placerville. Some

40 mule loads had been taken out and prepared for packing.

Next morning it was found that the pack train under Savariano had departed in the night. The lead had been covered up and has never been found since. The only thing ever seen or heard of the train was by an early teamster as it was filing towards the mountain by Woodford's, and beyond. Savariano had played Maldonado false, had stolen the mules and from $40,000 to $50,000 in ore, and left the country. Instead of going through by Placerville, he kept along the eastern slope of the mountains, struck down by Aurora, thence through Mono into Inyo county, California. It was during this flight that the gold mines of Cerro Gordo, in Inyo county, were discovered, and the white-haired Mexican said yesterday that Savariano was in that section now.

A year ago last summer, Mr. Moore saw a Mexican walking over the section where the old original Mexican claim lay. He watched the man for an hour, as he appeared to be searching for something, but seemed unable to find the bearings. At last Mr. Moore interviewed and found him to be Savariano. He was then searching for the lead from which this rich ore had been taken, and which, on the night of the flight, had been covered up. Savariano at that time asserted, as does the old white-haired Mexican who was with him while here and who went away with him, that the rich lode from which that ore was taken has never been discovered, but remains to-day on the Ophir ground as it was left at that time. Savariano, when here, tried to get a lease of the ground of the Ophir company, but did not succeed. The old Mexican says things have changed so that he cannot tell for sure where the lode lay, but that Savariano knows where it is, and can uncover it in a day or two.

There are several things which go to corroborate this wonderful story. The sudden disappearance of the Mexicans and their pack mules is well-known to all early Comstockers. This was followed by a cessation of work on the claim and desertion of the premises.

INDEX

A

107

H

Hale & Norcross Mine, 54-5, 88
Hale, Calvin, 54-5
Halleck, Nevada, 99
Hammack A.G., 31-32
Hannah, Thomas, 68
Hardenberg, J.R., 34
Harris, E.B., 74, 79
Harrison, B.A., 11
Harrold & Drynan Mine, 51-2
Harrold, John, 51-2
Hastings, Joseph, 34
Hayes, Jack, 28
Hearst, George, 13, 31, 40
Henderson, Alexander, 49, 50
Henderson, William, 49-50
Hillyer, M.C., 41
Holmes, James P., 50-1, 79
"Hope Mining Co.," 90
Houseworth, V.A., 13, 57-8
Howland, W.H., 73
Hudson, 50
Hughes, Francis J., 13
Humboldt, Baron Alexander Von, 99
Humboldt County, Nevada, 99
Humboldt River, 95, 99
Humboldt Route, 95, 100

I

Imperial Empire, see Empire Imperial
Imperial South Mine, 44
Jessup, John "Pike", 61-2
Johnson, J. Neely, 41

K

Keller Mill, 79
"Kentuck," see Osburn, John
Kentuck Mine, 33
Killala, Richard, 12
Kinney, George W., 61
Kinney, Mine, 61
Kirby, Joseph, 8

Knox, Israil W., 79

L

Lady Bryan Mine, 88
Lander County, Nevada, 99
Lander, Frederick W., 99
Lassen, Peter, 18
Las Vegas, Nevada, 97
Latrobe Mine, 89
Lauer, M., 15
Lee Mining District, Inyo County, California, 18
Lent, William M., 40
Lincoln County, Nevada, 98, 99
Logan & Holmes Mine, 50-1
Logan, Hugh, 50-1, 79
Lyon County, Nevada, 99
Lyon, Nathaniel, 99

M

McCreery, Andrew B., 41
McKinry, J., 41
McLaughlin, Patrick, 4, 13, 31
McNulty, William, 34, 79
Maldonado brothers (Francisco, Gabriel & Epistacio "Muchacho" Maldonado), 13, 59, 71, 104-5
Mayfield, Bill, 68-9
Mexican Mine, 3, 13, 33, 59, 61, 71, 105
Mill City, Nevada, 99
Mills, John H., 49
Moore, John L., 104-5
Mormons, 21, 34, 54, 100
Mormon Station, 95; see also Genoa, Nevada
Morrison, William, 13, 31, 40
Mosheimer & Kustel Mill (Joseph Mosheimer & Guido Kustel), 14
Mosheimer, Joseph, 79
Mount Davidson Mine, 88, 89
Muddy River, 95, 100
Murphy, John, 53-4

Spanish Mine, 59; see also
Mexican Mine
Sparrow, Erastus, 40-1, 66, 79
Sproul Mill, 79
Staples, Alpheus, 73, 79
Steptoe Route, 95
Stevenson, C.C., 74
Stewart, William M., 68
Stone & Gates' Crossing, 11
Stone, John F., 11
Storey, Edward, 99
Storey County, Nevada, 99
Strong, Charles L., 84
"Sucker Mining Co.," 90
Swansea Mill, 66

T

Tahoe, 97
Thompson, William N., 41
Toano, Nevada, 99
Toiyabe Mountains, 98, 100
Toquima Mountains, 98
Trench & Sparrow Mill, 66, 79
Trench & Sparrow Mine, 66
Trench, Joseph, 66, 79
Trench Mine, 44, 66
Triglone, John, 65-6
Triglone Mine, 44, 65-6
Truckee River, 11, 27, 28, 95, 97
Twin River Mining District, 53, 100
Twin Rivers, 100
Tyler process of amalgamation, 85

U

Utah Mine, 59, 88

V

Verdi, Nevada, 99
Veatch process of amalgamation, 85
Virginia City, Nevada, 4, 5, 7, 15, 20, 23, 27, 29, 30, 31, 46, 59, 65, 71, 79, 89, 92, 96
Virginia Ledge (Lode), 3, 4, 92
Vista, Nevada, 99

W

Wadsworth, Nevada, 99
Walker, Joseph, 100
Walker Lake, 100
Walker River, 95, 100
Walsh & Woodworth Mill, 78-9
Walsh, James, 10, 11, 13, 14, 15, 19, 31, 37, 39-40, 57, 58, 79, 81
Washoe County, Nevada, 97, 98
Washoe Gold and Silver Mining Co., 72
Washoe Indians, 97
Washoe process of amalgamation, 71-74, 77, 81, 83, 85
Washoe Valley, 32, 45, 54, 82, 95, 97
Webb, Joseph, 49
Wells, Nevada, 99
White, Alexander, 53
White & Murphy Mine, 53-4, 61
White Pine County, Nevada, 99
White Pine Mining District, 40, 51, 52, 53, 99
White Plains, Nevada, 99
White River, 100
Williams brothers, 25
Wilson, J. Downes, 40, 79
Winnemucca, Chief, 98
Winnemucca, Lake, 98
Winnemucca, Nevada, 98
Winters, John B., 79
Winters, John D., 31-32
Winters, Joseph, 13, 31-2
Winters, Theodore, 31-2
Woodford's, California, 105
Woodworth, Joseph, 13, 15, 37, 39-40, 78-9

Y

Yellow Jacket Mine, 32, 55, 58